Copyright @ 2024 Author
Shaneque Murray-Johnson
Independent Publishing
All rights reserved.

No part of this publication may be reproduced, distributed, or transmitted in any form or by any means, including photocopying, recording, or other electronic or mechanical methods, without the prior written permission of the publisher, except in the case of brief quotations embodied in critical reviews and certain other noncommercial uses permitted by copyright law.

ISBN: 9798339949947

Once upon a time, there was a dog whose name was Danny. He was known as a Jamaican brown terrier. When Danny was born, he had a very exciting childhood. His mother loved him and his eleven siblings very much, but she was very fond of Danny. As time went by, Danny realized that on random days strangers would come into the yard, and one by one, his brothers were taken until there were only four.

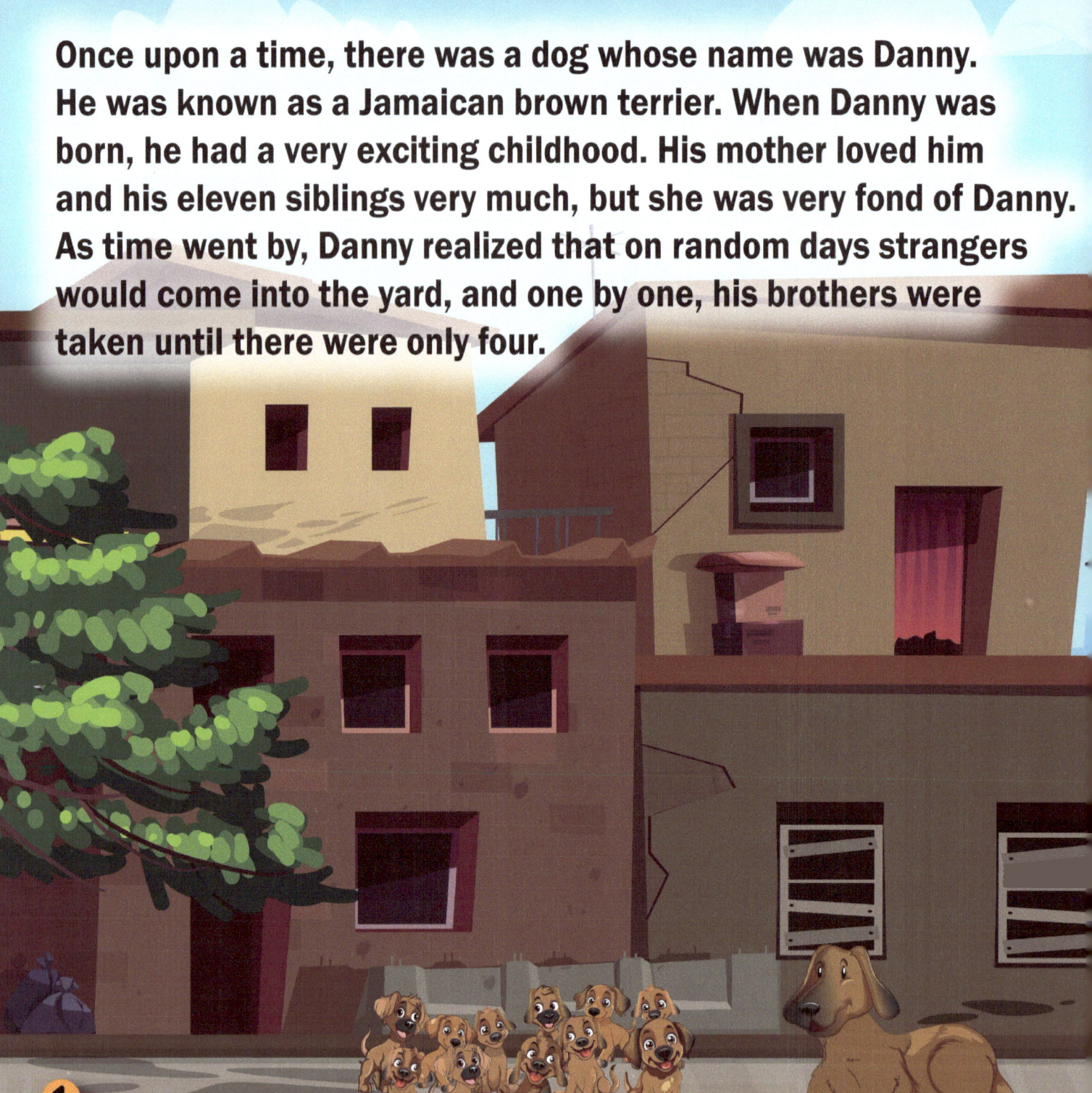

Danny belonged to a little girl named Sheila. She loved to play with Danny and feed him. Danny's favourite pastime was watching the little picture box through Sheila's window. He later learnt that this was a television. One day, Danny saw a movie all about dogs. He said to his mother, "Mom, one day I'm gonna go to a doggy salon, wear a doggy jacket, and be real famous!" Danny's brothers laughed at him. But his Mom smiled and said, "Danny, anything is possible, if you believe." Danny never forgot his mother's words.

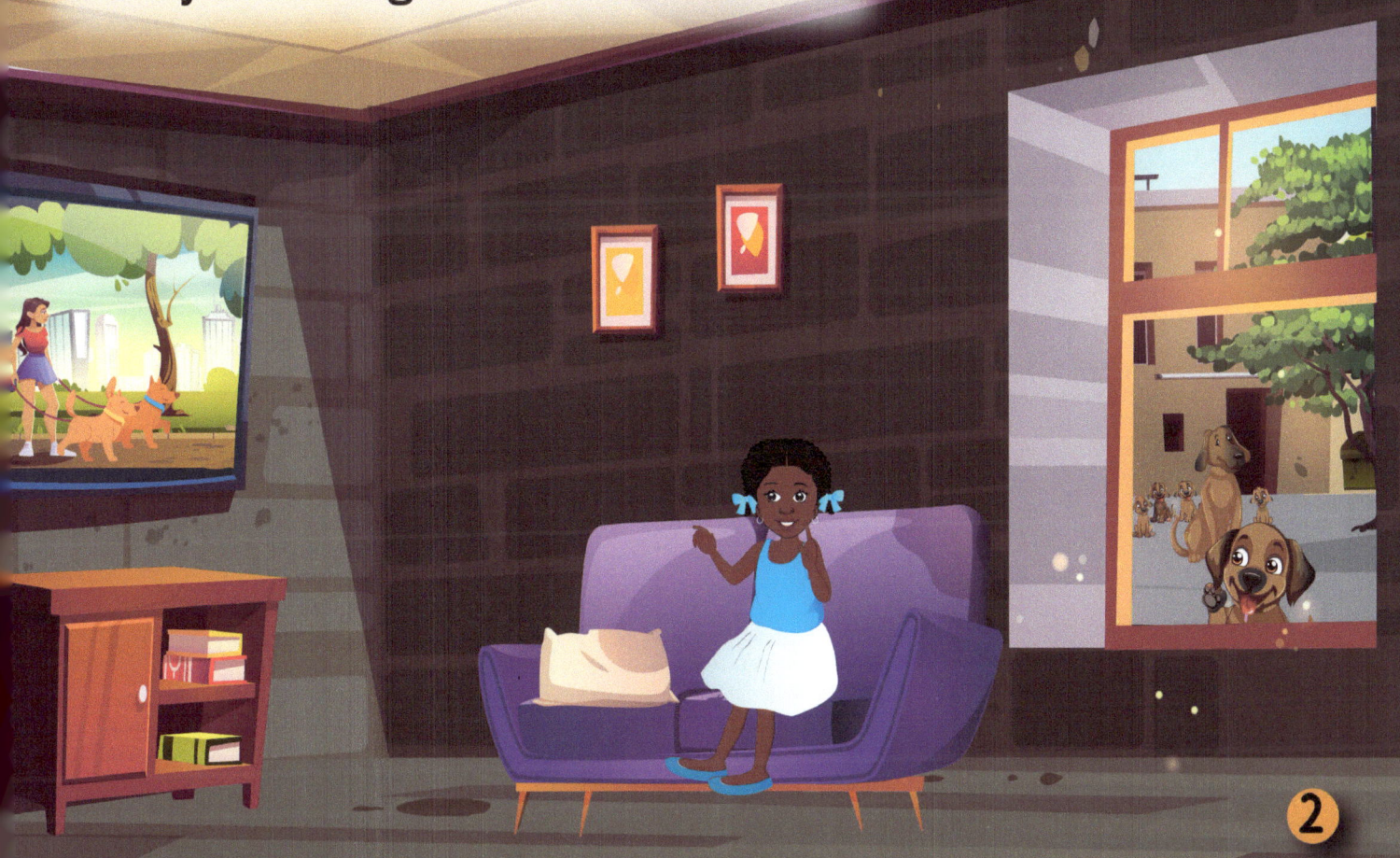

One day, Danny's mother went out and did not return. Three days had passed, and Danny and his brothers were worried. Then, Danny overheard Sheila's mom saying a car had hit his mom. Danny was saddened. And little did he know that things were about to change. That very day, a big orange power truck came, and Danny heard people arguing and talking loudly. Then, in the night, he realized the television was not turned on and the building was in complete darkness.

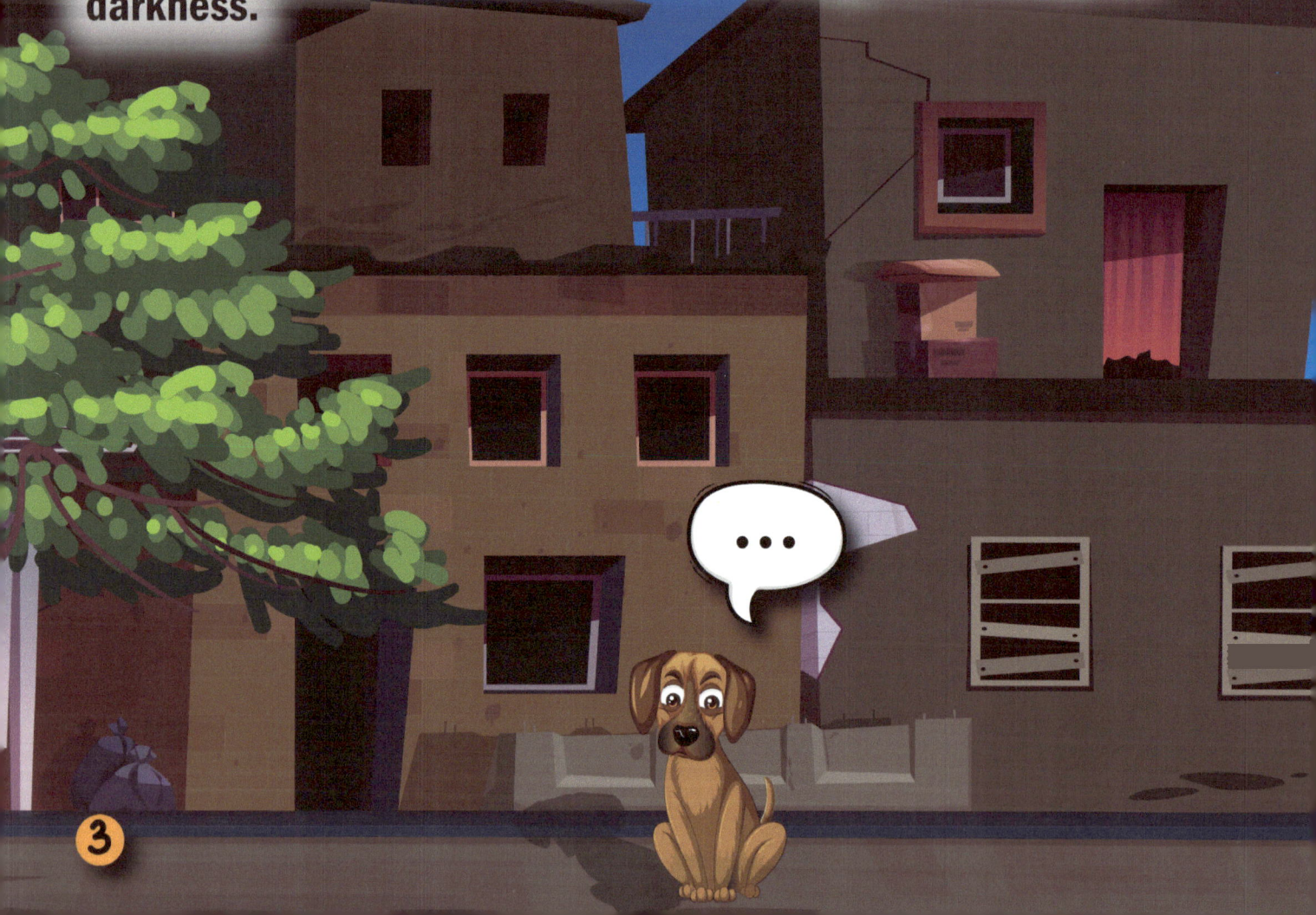

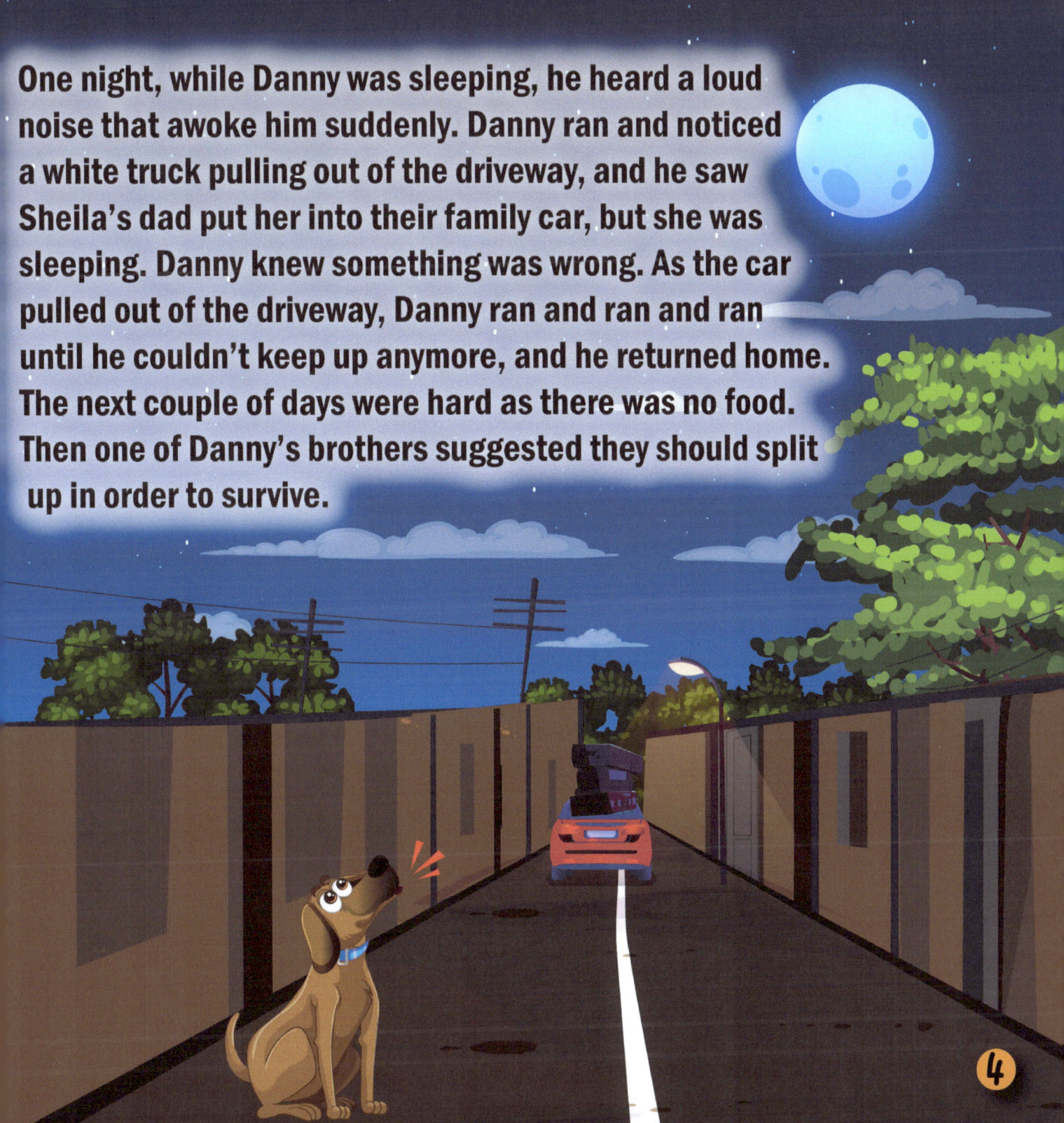

One night, while Danny was sleeping, he heard a loud noise that awoke him suddenly. Danny ran and noticed a white truck pulling out of the driveway, and he saw Sheila's dad put her into their family car, but she was sleeping. Danny knew something was wrong. As the car pulled out of the driveway, Danny ran and ran and ran until he couldn't keep up anymore, and he returned home. The next couple of days were hard as there was no food. Then one of Danny's brothers suggested they should split up in order to survive.

Each of Danny's brothers left, and he was all alone. Danny began to reflect as he looked through the window where the television was in Sheila's house. He remembered Sheila's smiles and her laughter as they played. Danny remembered the movie he had seen that was all about dogs, and his mother's voice resounded in his head, "Danny, anything is possible if you believe." So Danny set out, determined to live this doggy dream.

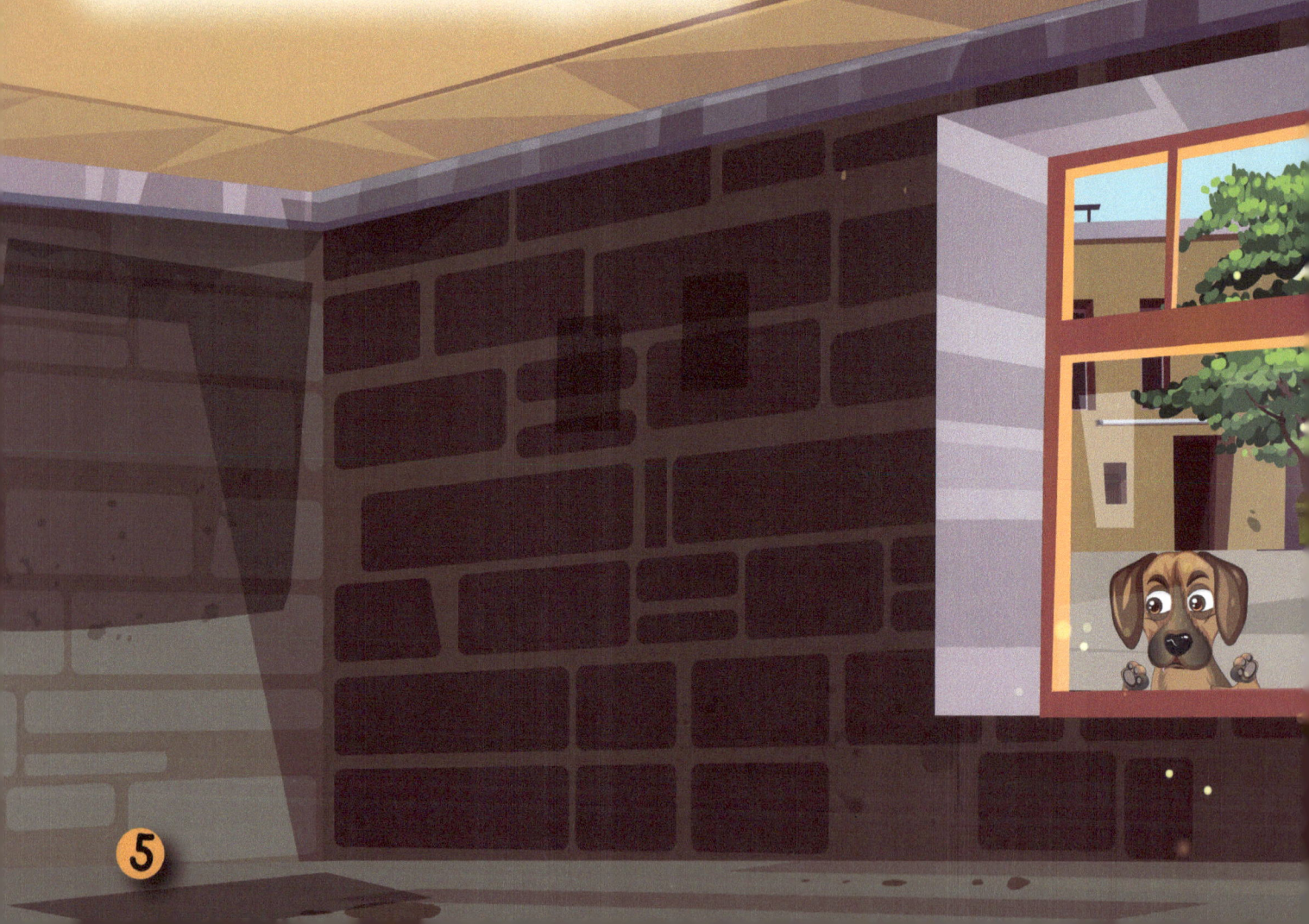

Danny wandered from place to place. He had to learn how to survive "in the wild." He quickly learnt that the world was not a dog's friend. He would sometimes be walking, and suddenly a sharp rock would hit him, and when he would look, there would be some unruly boys playing, and he would be their target. He would have to run very fast in order to save his skin. There were times when Danny had to run to avoid being hit by a car as he crossed the road.

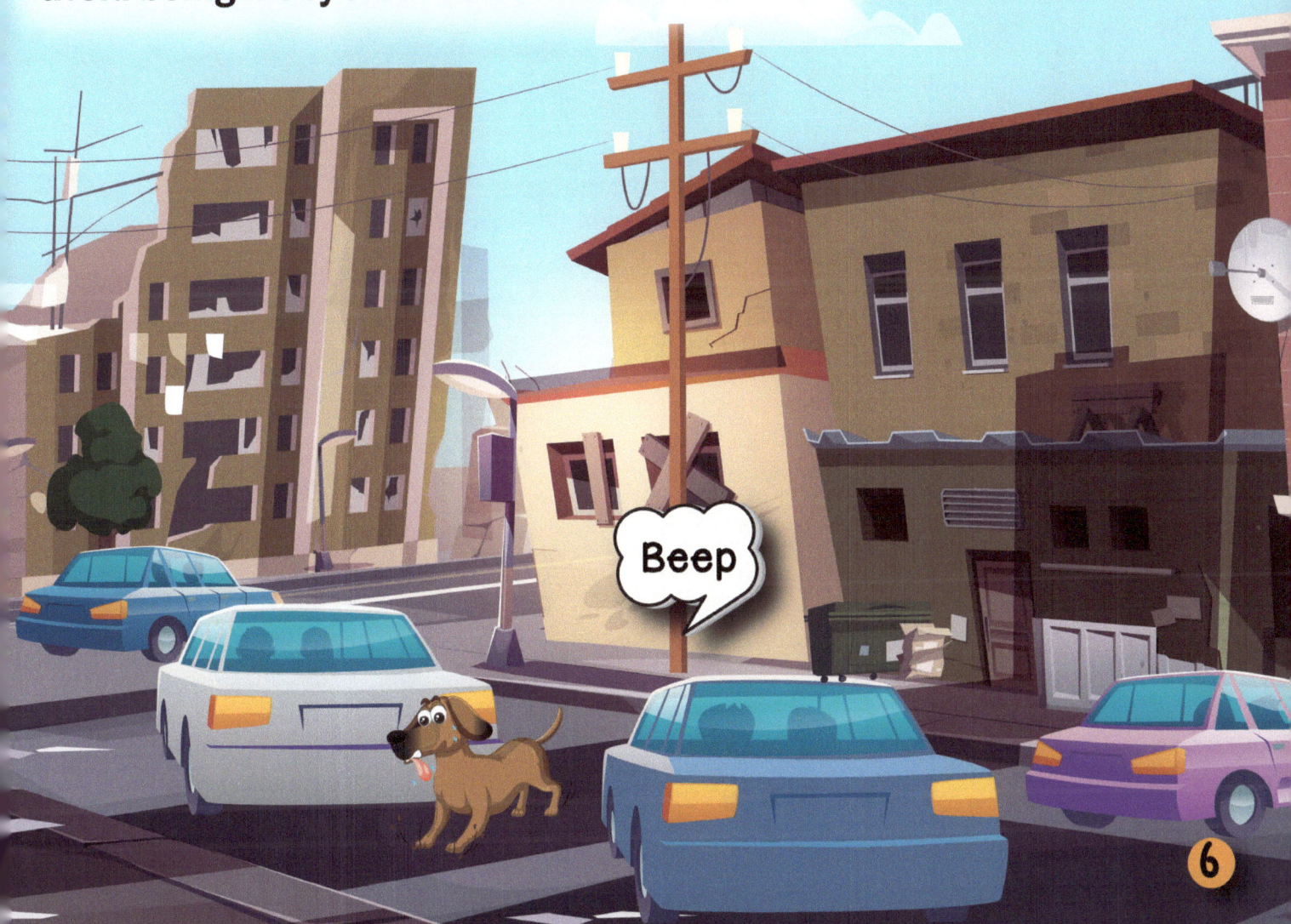

Then Danny met a group of animals—dogs and cats—who called themselves The Jammings. They hung out by the dumps at a restaurant by night. They shared meals and laughed as each dog told adventurous stories about their day. But they warned Danny that in the day he had to go walk the streets or he would get in trouble with the owners.

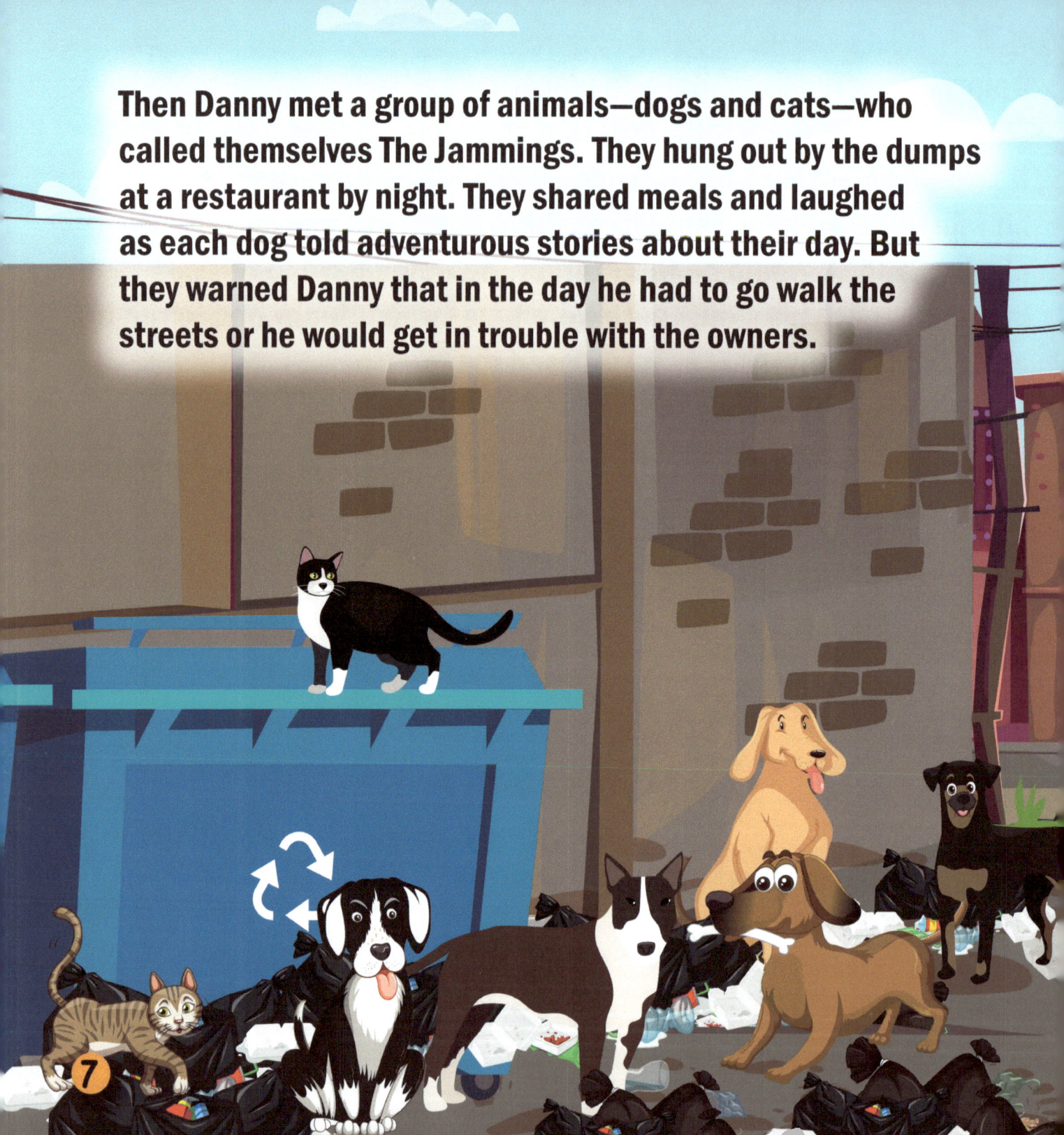

So during the days, Danny would walk through neighborhoods and the marketplace, always being careful. One day, Danny was so hungry that he saw a lady eating and went up to her, staring. The woman pretended to throw food for Danny, and every time Danny would jump in anticipation, the woman would laugh. Then suddenly, a man came out of nowhere and threw a stone. Danny did not see it coming, and Danny was badly injured. He crept into a corner and wept bitterly. By this, Danny was starving and spotted a banana peel nearby. Danny began to nibble at it.

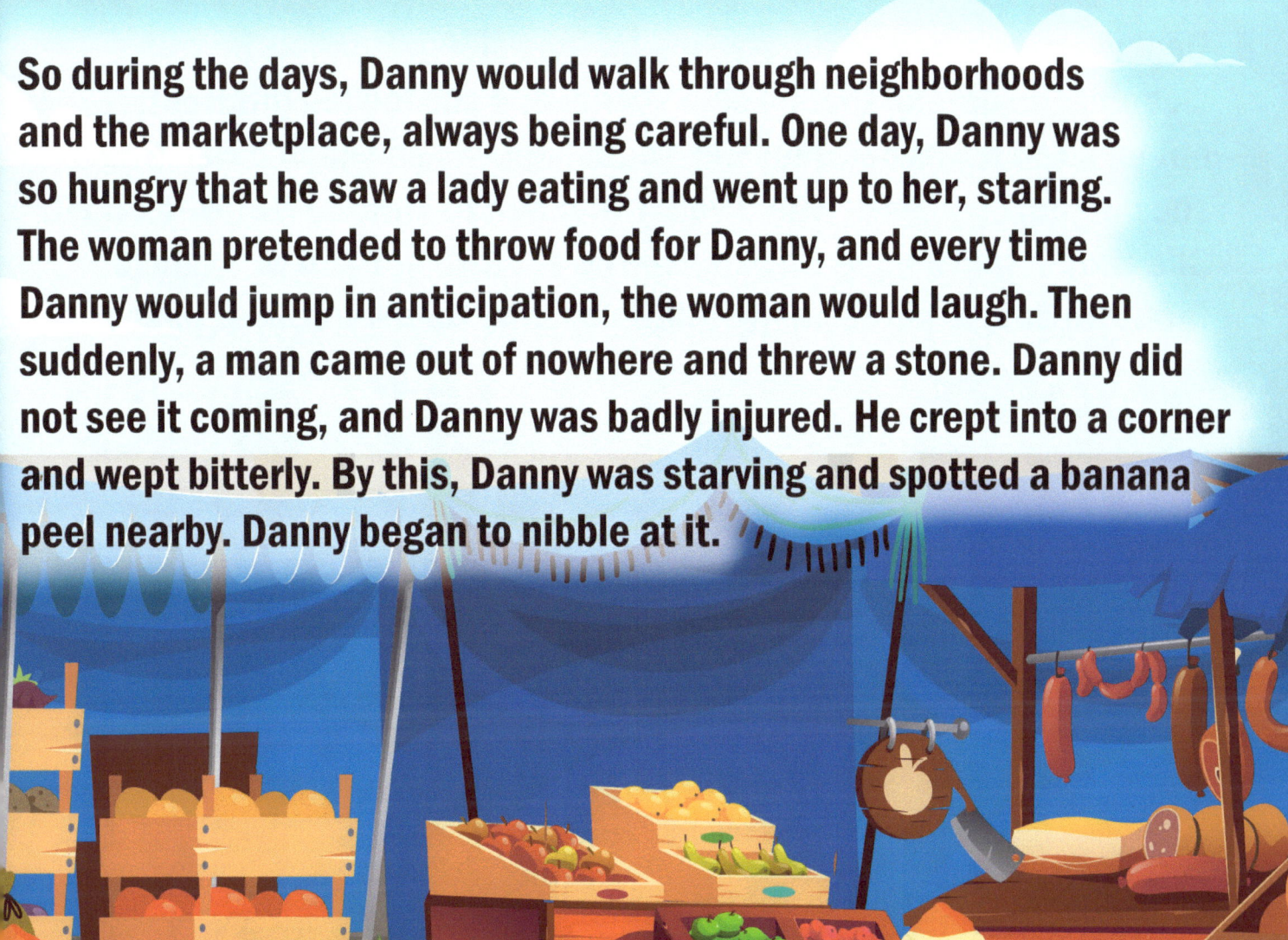

Danny was hungry and thirsty, and he fell asleep. Then, as he was sleeping, he dreamt that he saw Sheila, and she looked different, but he knew it was her. They were both happy to see each other, and she put him on a leash with a collar that had the letters D-A-N-N-Y on it. She bought him doggie clothes, and he sat with her and watched his favourite doggie movie on the television, and Danny felt so at peace.

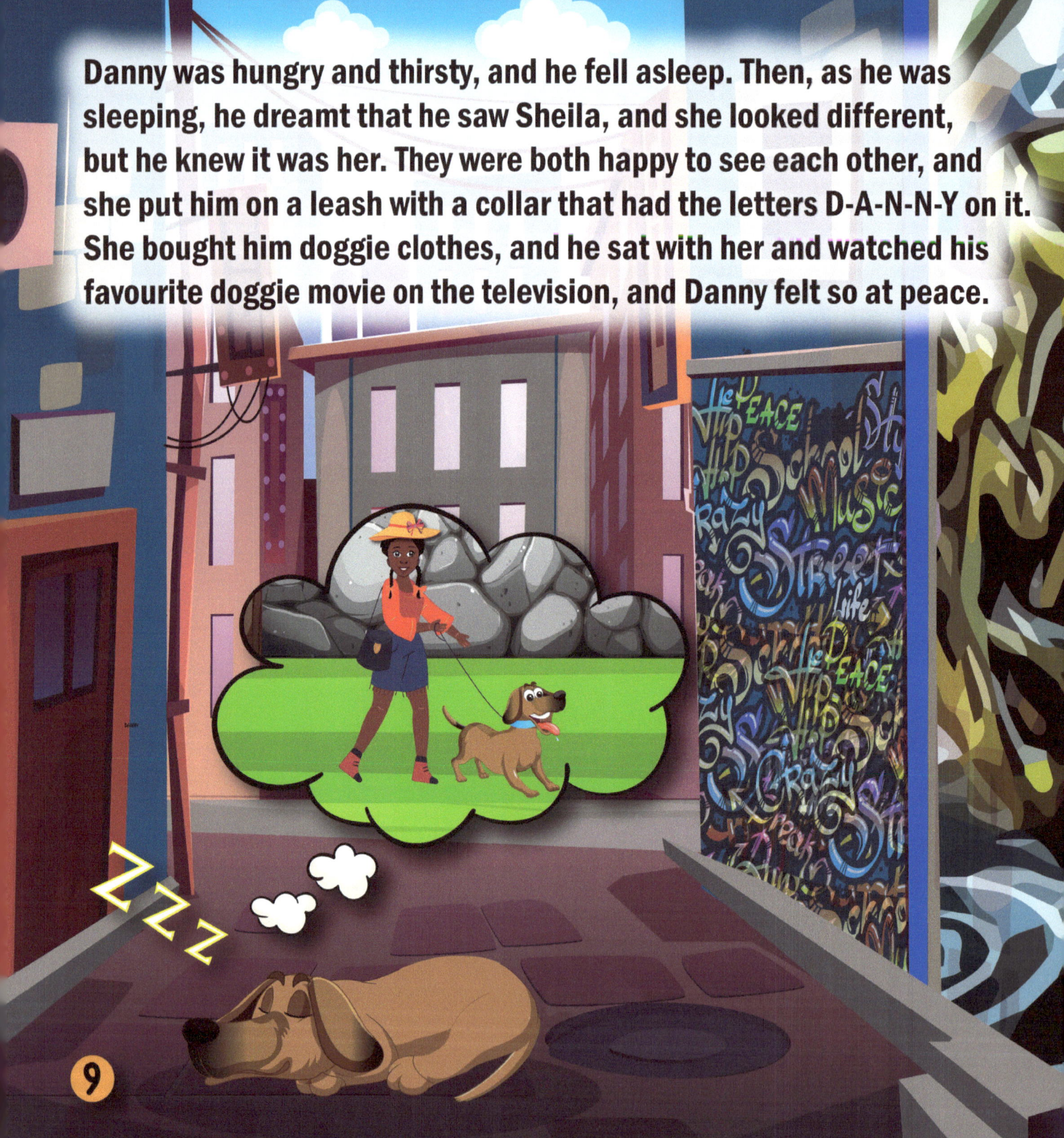

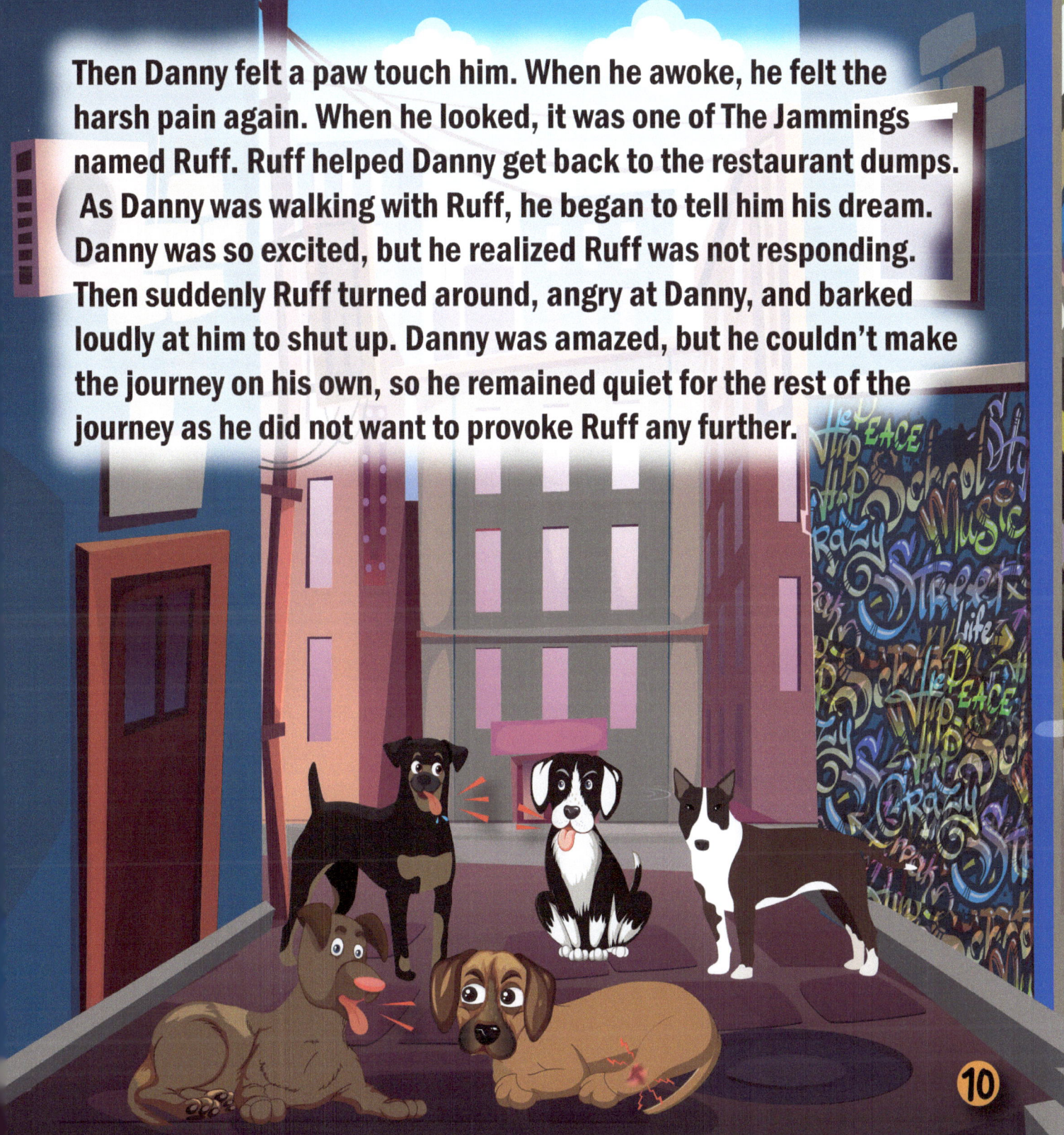

Then Danny felt a paw touch him. When he awoke, he felt the harsh pain again. When he looked, it was one of The Jammings named Ruff. Ruff helped Danny get back to the restaurant dumps. As Danny was walking with Ruff, he began to tell him his dream. Danny was so excited, but he realized Ruff was not responding. Then suddenly Ruff turned around, angry at Danny, and barked loudly at him to shut up. Danny was amazed, but he couldn't make the journey on his own, so he remained quiet for the rest of the journey as he did not want to provoke Ruff any further.

When Danny arrived, one of The Jammings handed him a bite to eat, and Danny sadly pulled himself into a corner, where he fell asleep. The next day, he heard Ruff shouting, "Hey, Danny the dreamer, wake up; it's time to go!" All The Jammings left, but Danny was in so much pain that he decided to remain in a corner. The restaurant owner came out to throw something away, and he saw Danny. He shouted at him and told him to leave, but to the man's surprise, Danny did not move. So he took up a pebble and threw it at Danny. Danny tried to stand up, but he could not make it. The man noticed Danny was injured, so he went back inside and left him. Then Danny saw the man returning. This time, the man brought food and water, set before Danny, and went back inside. Danny stayed there all day until The Jammings returned.

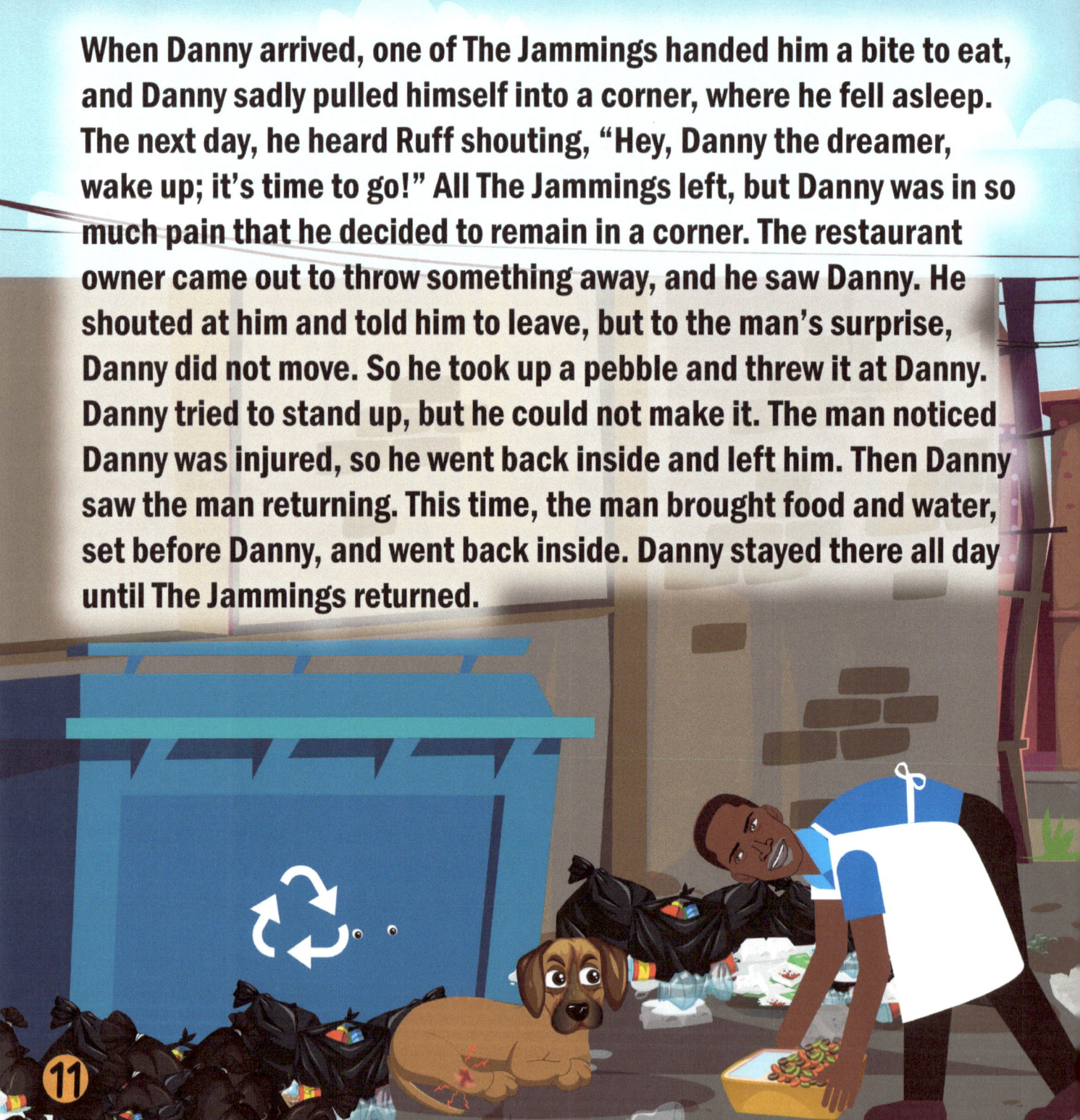

When they came back, they realized Danny was in the same spot. Ruff said, "Hey, dreamer boy, why didn't you leave?" Danny explained that he was in pain and couldn't move. He told them about the man from the restaurant and tried to convince The Jammings that humans weren't so bad after all. Once again, Ruff got upset and told Danny to shut up with all that human talk. Then Ruff continued, "Listen, Dreamer Boy, I don't know where you came from; I have been in these streets. Dogs don't have happy endings. My mom died while I was a pup; she got hit by a car. I had a brother, and just like you, he trusted humans. They fed him and took care of him. But one day they set him up to fight a bully, a much bigger dog than he was, and I watched as that dog defeated my brother as the humans cheered. When it was all over, he was dead. I've been in these streets; you need to wake up and stop all this talk about dogs wearing clothes. These streets aren't safe and humans are bad news!" All The Jammings cheered when Ruff was through talking. Danny remained quiet.

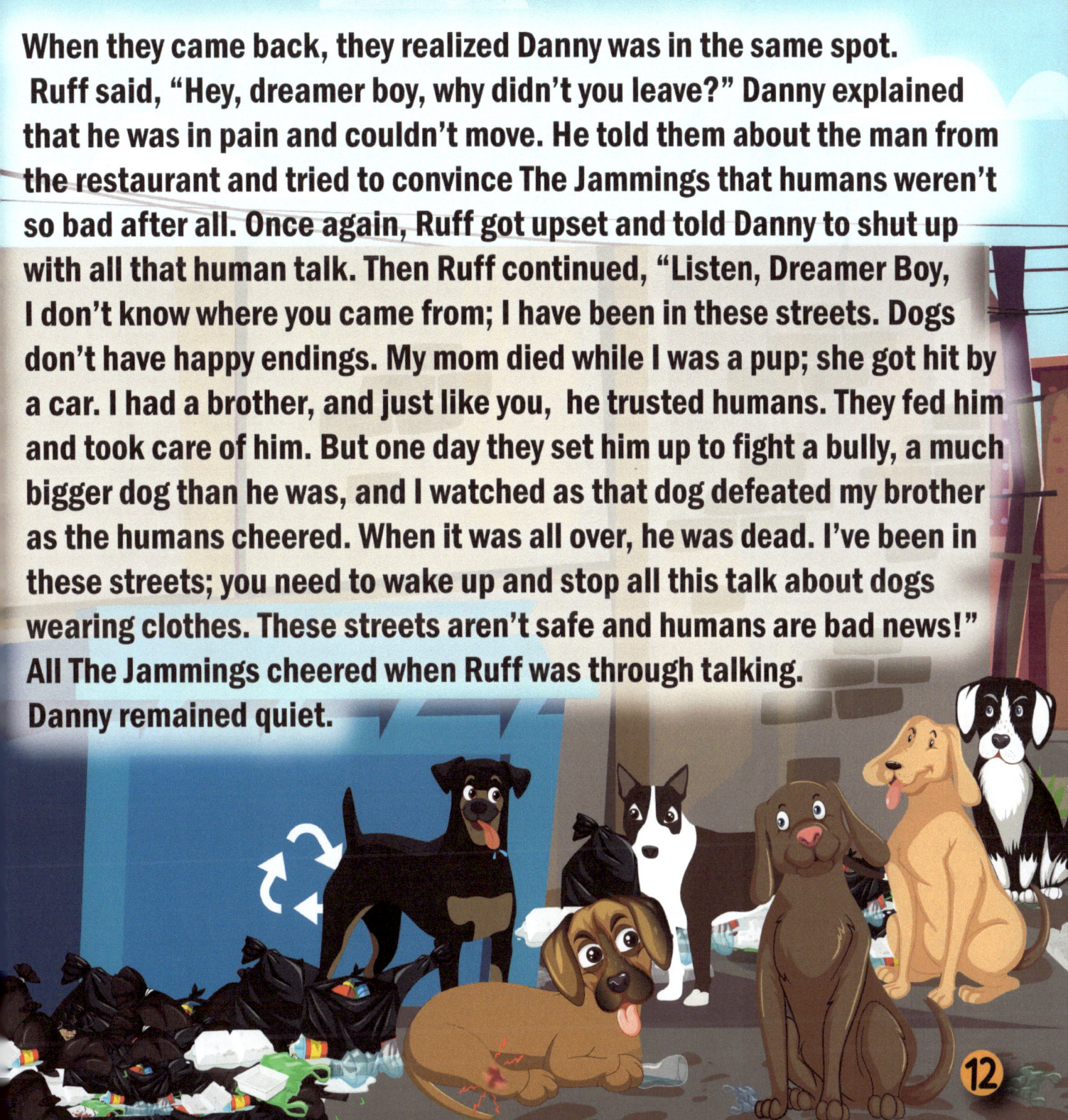

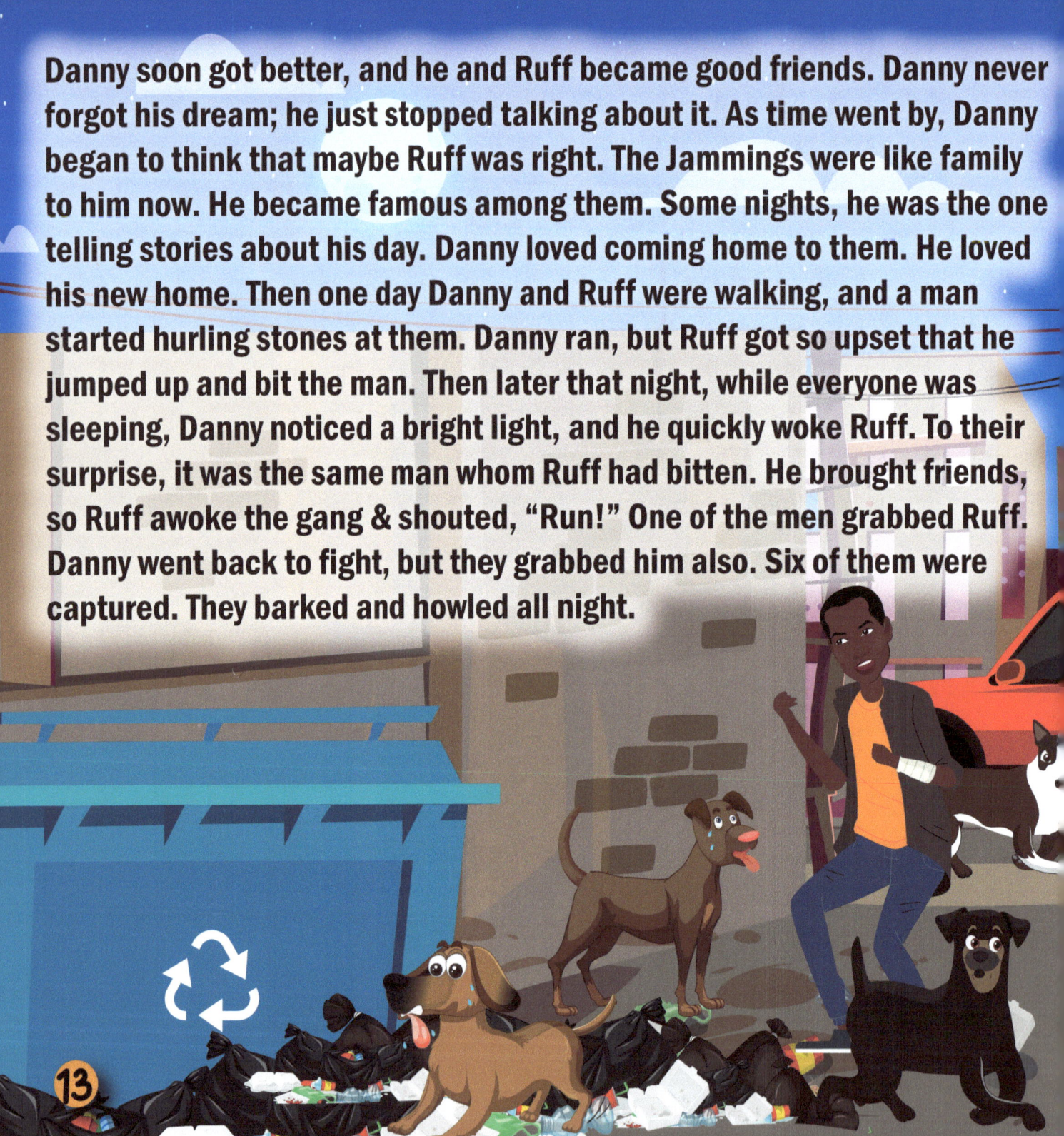

Danny soon got better, and he and Ruff became good friends. Danny never forgot his dream; he just stopped talking about it. As time went by, Danny began to think that maybe Ruff was right. The Jammings were like family to him now. He became famous among them. Some nights, he was the one telling stories about his day. Danny loved coming home to them. He loved his new home. Then one day Danny and Ruff were walking, and a man started hurling stones at them. Danny ran, but Ruff got so upset that he jumped up and bit the man. Then later that night, while everyone was sleeping, Danny noticed a bright light, and he quickly woke Ruff. To their surprise, it was the same man whom Ruff had bitten. He brought friends, so Ruff awoke the gang & shouted, "Run!" One of the men grabbed Ruff. Danny went back to fight, but they grabbed him also. Six of them were captured. They barked and howled all night.

When they woke up in the morning, they were each in cages. Danny noticed a foul smell in the place. He saw other animals as well. Danny asked one of the pigs what manner of place it was. The pig grunted, "This is the butcher house, they feed you, and you eat. Every day strangers come through here; if they pick you, then the butcher takes you there," and he pointed. Then Danny and Ruff looked in the direction where he pointed and were terrified.

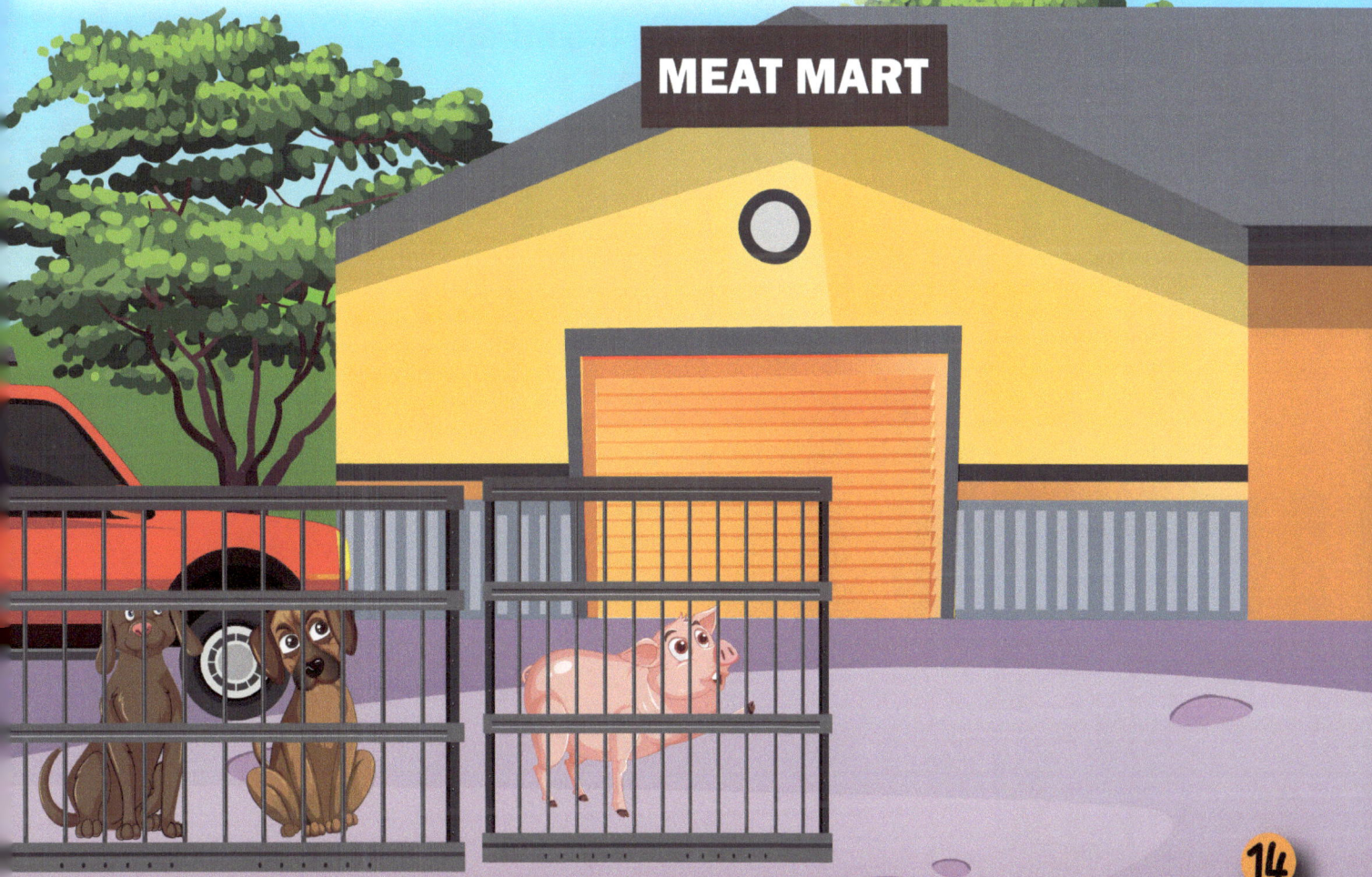

Days passed, and one by one, the cages would be empty, and then by the next day, they would be full again. There wasn't time to build a relationship with the animals. Danny began to reflect on when he was younger, the days he played with Sheila, the television through the window, and The Jammings, and he began to get sad. Then one day, the butcher came in and opened the goat cages and a few of the dog cages. So Danny summoned Ruff and the other dogs and told them he had a plan. When the butcher got to them, he released all six of them, and they walked in a straight line from the butcher's house to the yard. Then on their way, Danny bit one of the goats on his tail while nobody was looking. Then there was a big commotion as all the goats began to run to and fro. Danny then shouted, "Now!" All six dogs began to run; however, the butcher caught three of them. But Danny was glad Ruff made it out.

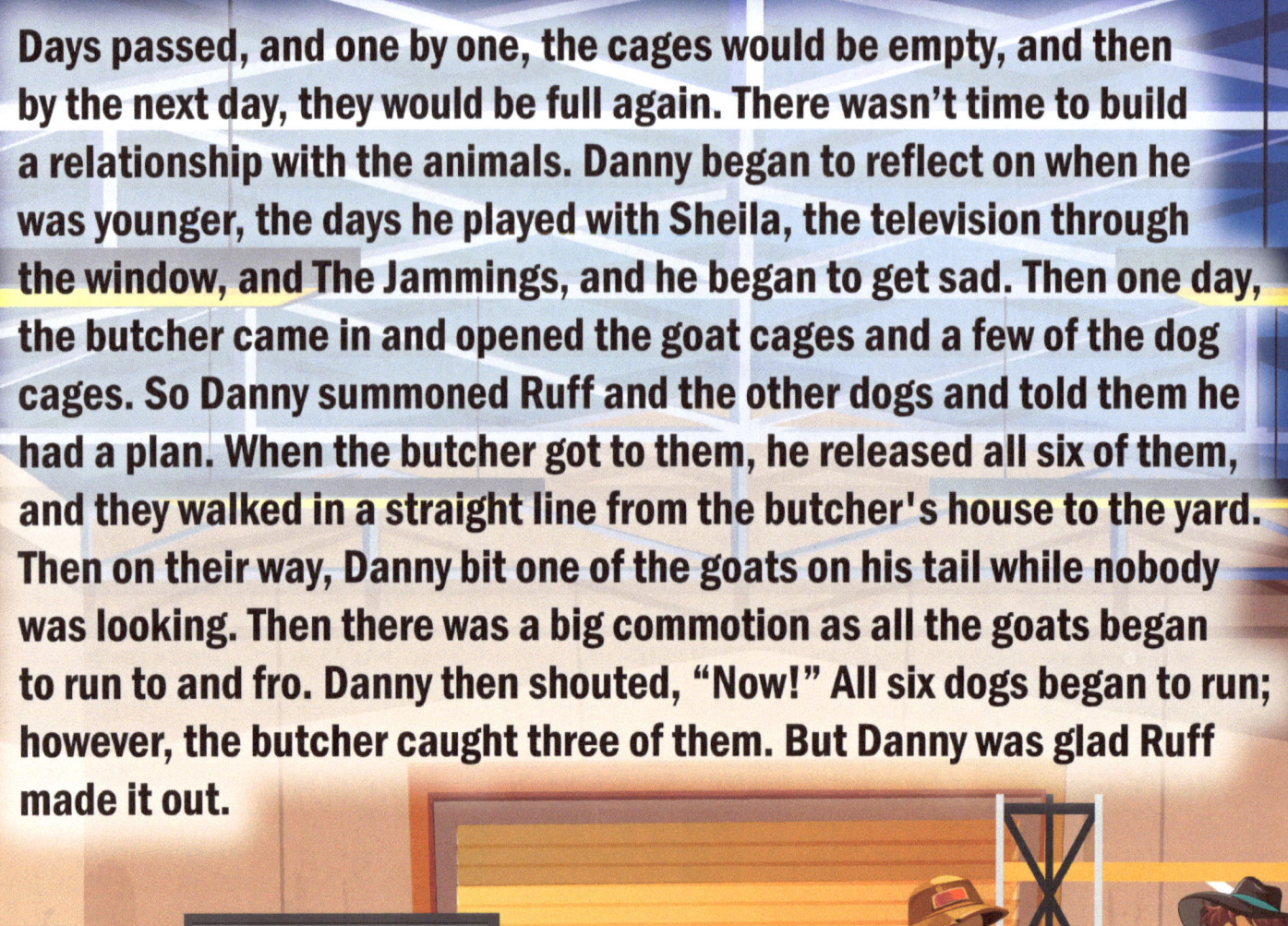

The other dog named Pet asked, "Shouldn't we go back for the others?" Ruff responded, "No, it's too dangerous; we may not make it out." Pet frowned. Ruff turned to Danny and said, "Good job, dreamer boy!" So the three started out on their journey. They went from place to place, and every night, they slept in a new place. Then one day, they came to a nice community with large gates. They snuck in past the guards. They rummaged through garbage bins daily. Danny was very happy, and it reminded him of when he was little.

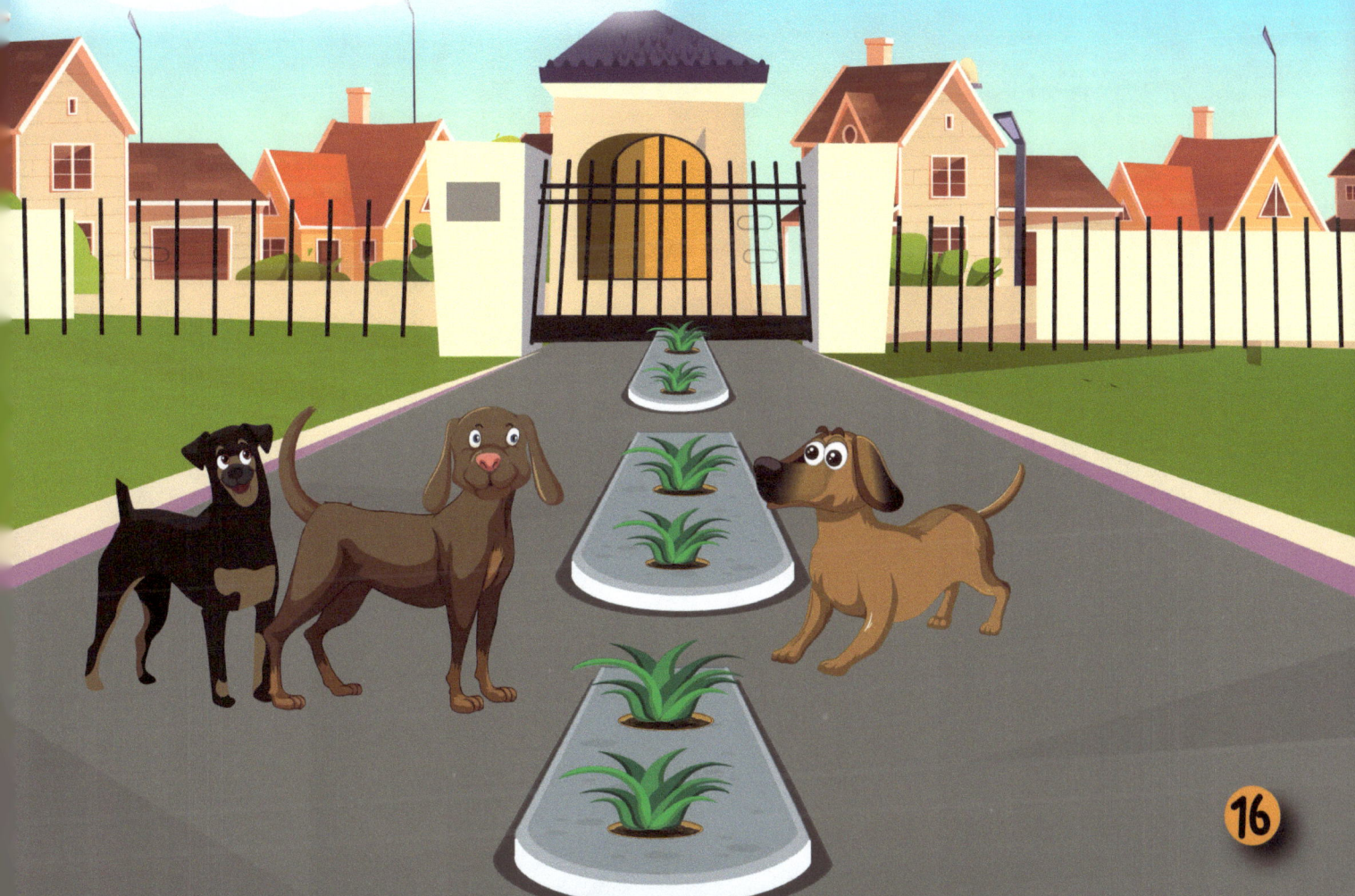

One night Danny called Ruff and said, "Come look," he brought him up to one of the windows. They both watched the television through the window. Sometimes Ruff would burst into laughter and suddenly catch himself. He reassured Danny that that kind of thing only happened in televisions. Sometime after, they found out Pet was with child and could not move around as freely. So she hid in a shaded area, and Danny and Ruff would go out, find food, and take it back for her. Then the day came when Pet gave birth to nine pups.

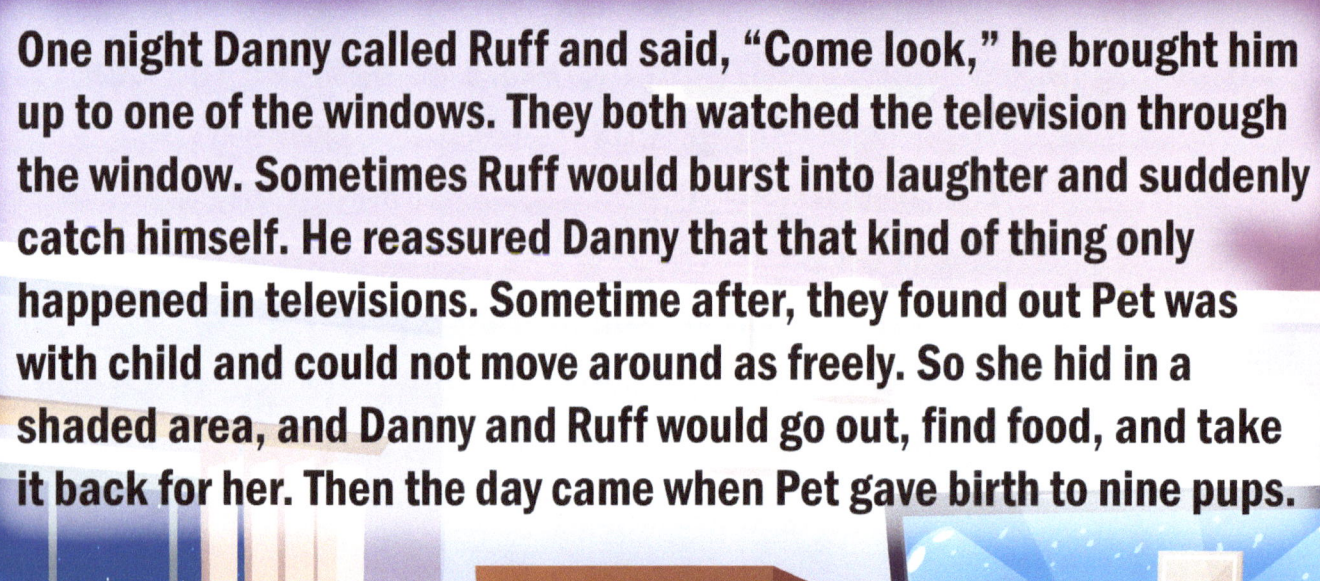

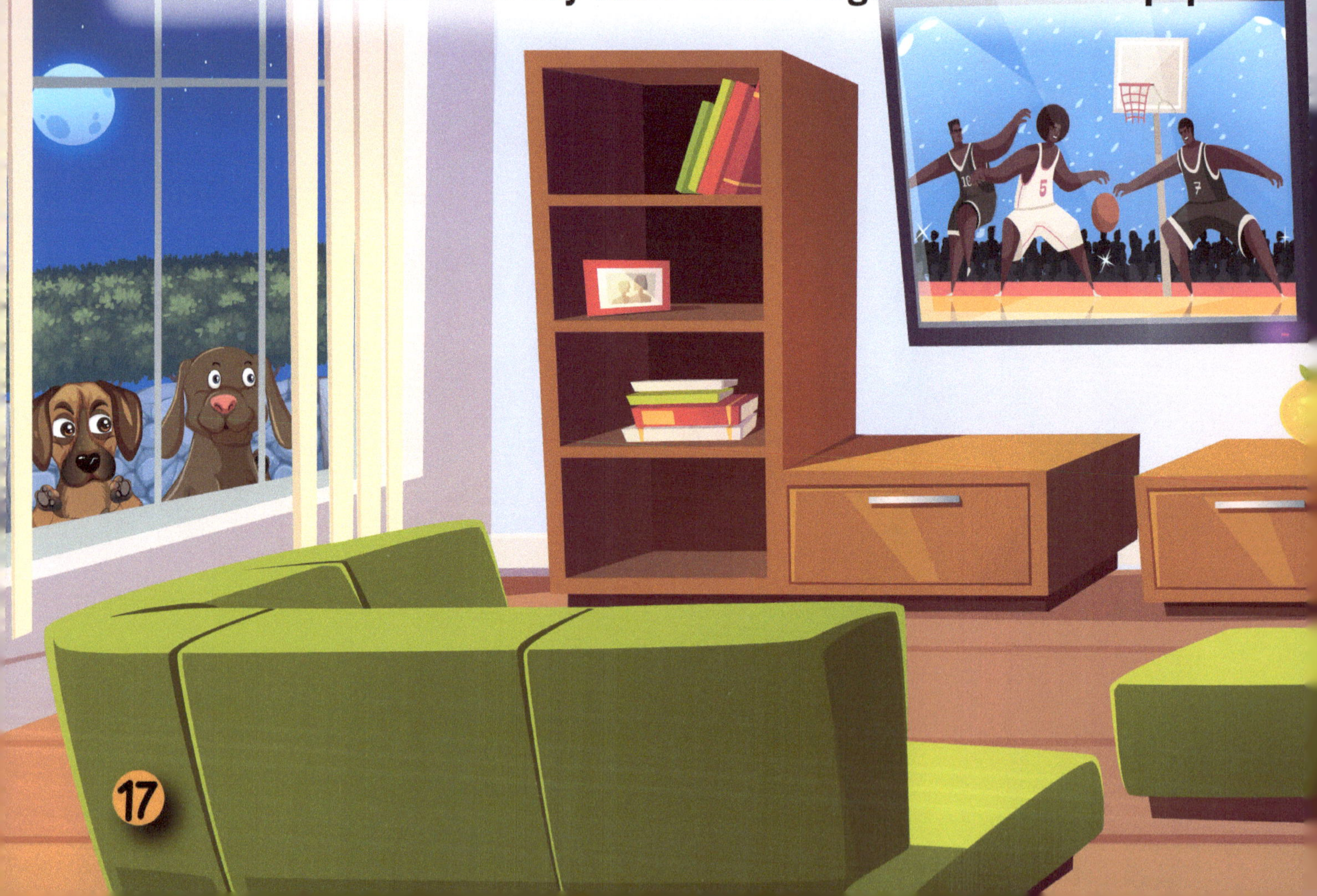

Danny was very happy. Ruff went aside to be alone with his thoughts. Danny followed him and asked what was wrong. Ruff responded, "Look around you, dreamer boy; this won't last. And these innocent pups might have to grow up and live the life I lived. This ain't no life for a dog." Danny replied, "Ruff, life has taught me to live in the moment. There's a time for everything! But don't miss out on happy moments sulking over the past. Before you know it, this moment would have passed, and you would have missed it. When it is time to be sad, be sad. But when it is time to be happy, be happy, and be very happy!" Danny signaled Ruff, and they both walked back over to Pet and the babies.

The next day, as they went out for food and returned, they saw two strange men standing over Pet and the pups. Ruff told Danny to be quiet, and they observed what the men were doing. They could hear Pet howling in the distance, as she was protecting the pups. Then the two men walked away. Ruff and Danny walked over to Pet, but they realized all the pups were still there. They asked Pet if she understood what the men were saying, but she did not.

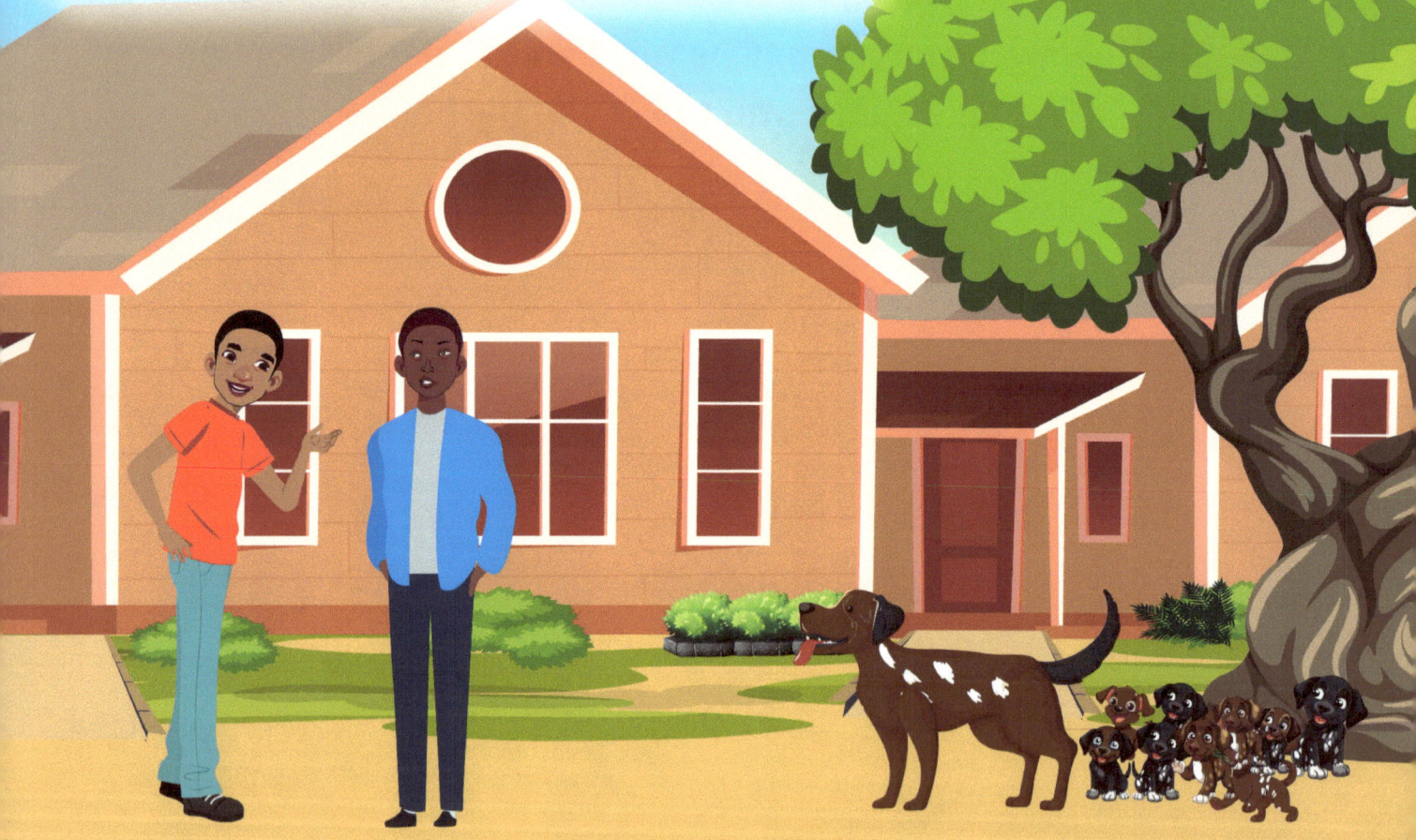

A few days passed, and they went back to their routines. The pups even got big enough to move around. So some nights, Danny would take one or two of the pups so they could watch television with him. Whenever the pups experienced the television, they would go back and tell the other pups. Then all the pups would get excited, and each pup wanted to go see. Ruff got up and called Danny aside.

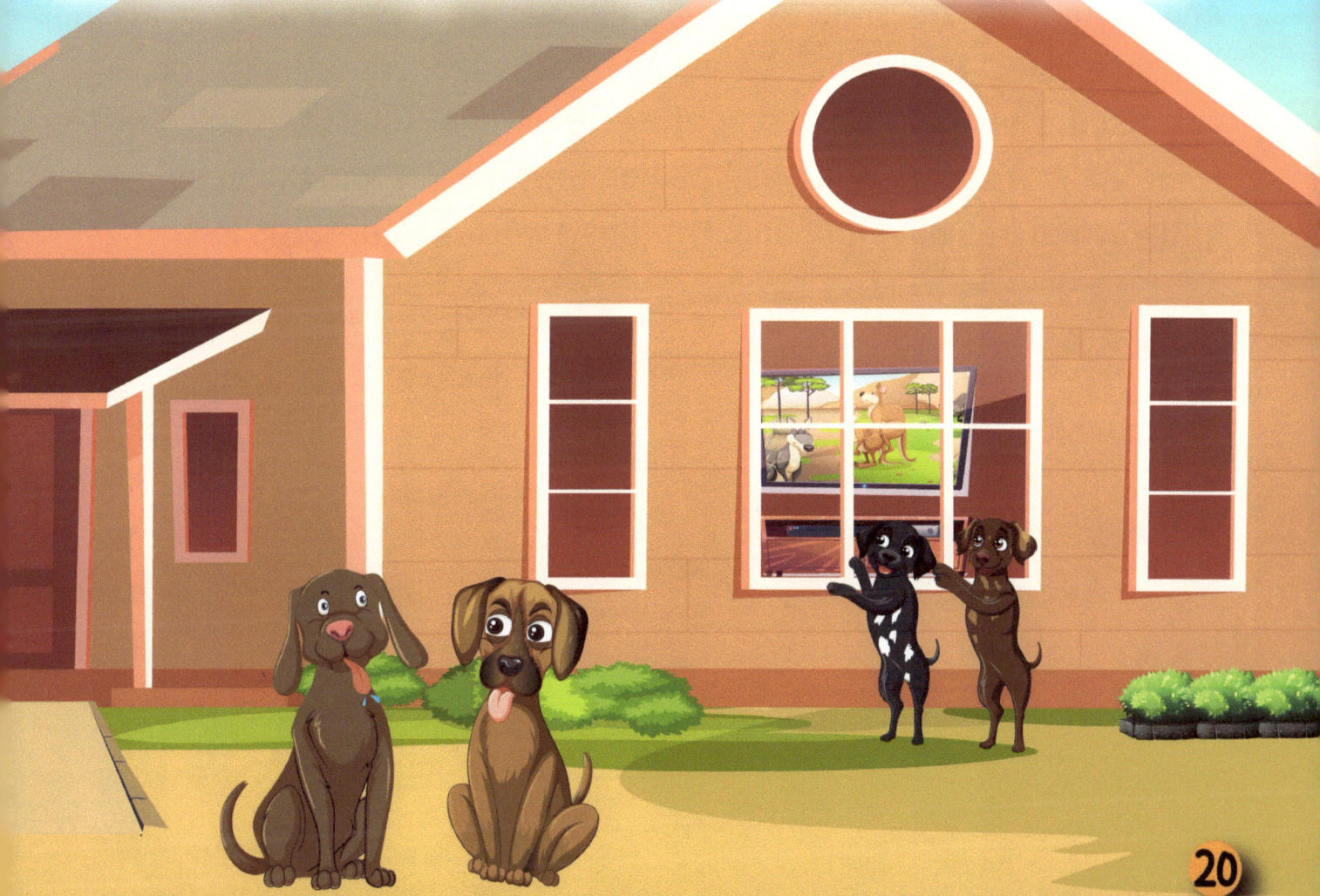

Ruff said to Danny, "Dreamer boy, things are good now, real good. But don't be filling these pups up with all that junk on the television. You and I know that these things don't happen in real life." Danny looked out into the distance, and he replied, "Ruff, every time I felt like giving up, it was my dream that kept me going. I'd rather give these kids a dream and send them out with something to fight for, than show them a world with no hope and send them out already defeated . I don't know about you, Ruff, but something down inside me keeps telling me dreams do come true." Ruff struck Danny across the face, and Danny was so surprised. The two struggled fighting for a while. Then they both noticed something. A white truck was heading towards Pet and the pups. They both looked at each other and, without a word, ran towards Pet.

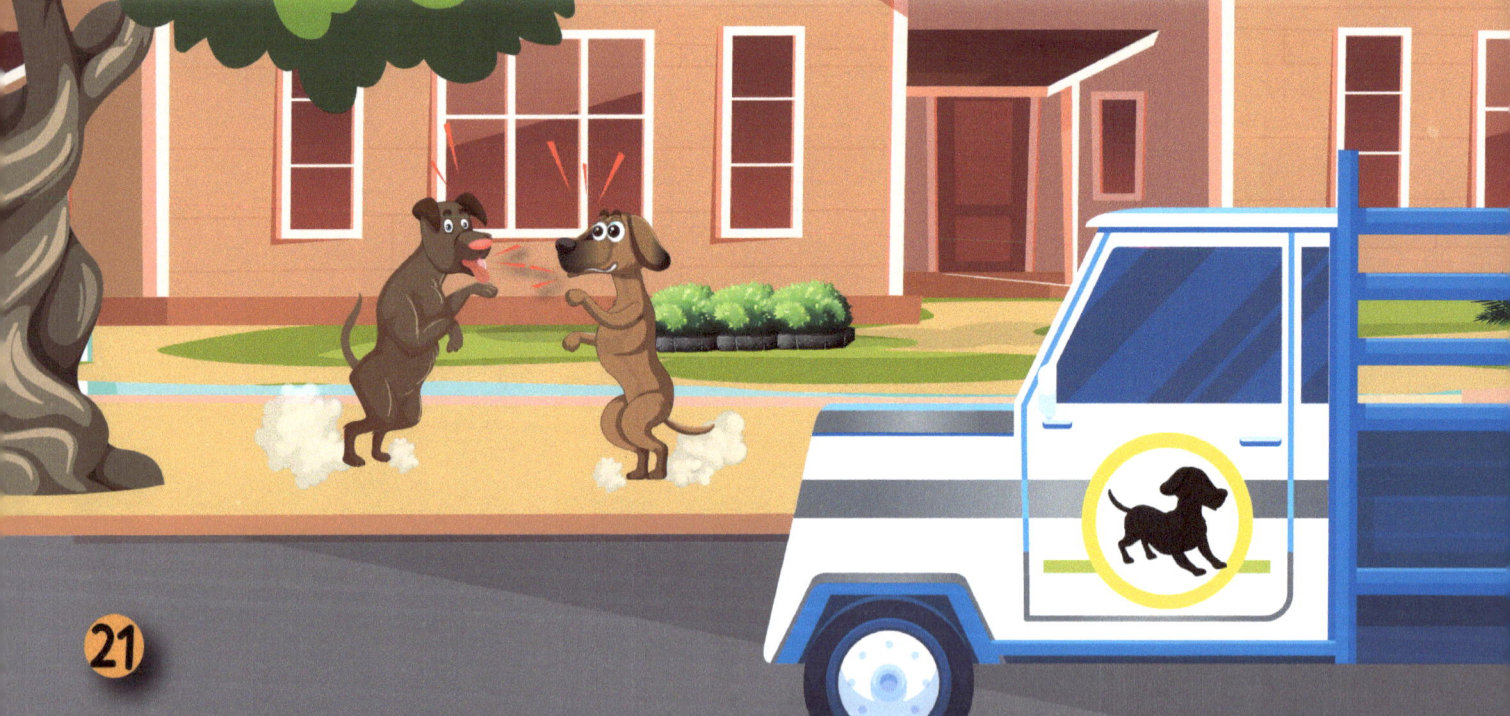

They outran the truck, woke Pet up, and gathered all the pups. The truck came to a stop right where they were, and some men with nets jumped out. The men began to call the pups; one by one, the pups went, and they put them into the truck. But Ruff and Danny each took one by the neck and ran and summoned Pet. Pet cried loudly, "No, I have to go get my pups!" Danny looked back at Ruff, dropped the pup he had taken in his mouth, and said, "Take care, Ruff; I'ma help Pet." Danny then jumped into the truck. Ruff ran! Then, when the men came back, they came with the two pups that Ruff had taken. Pet and Danny were sad as they did not know what lay at the end of this journey, and they did not know what had become of Ruff.

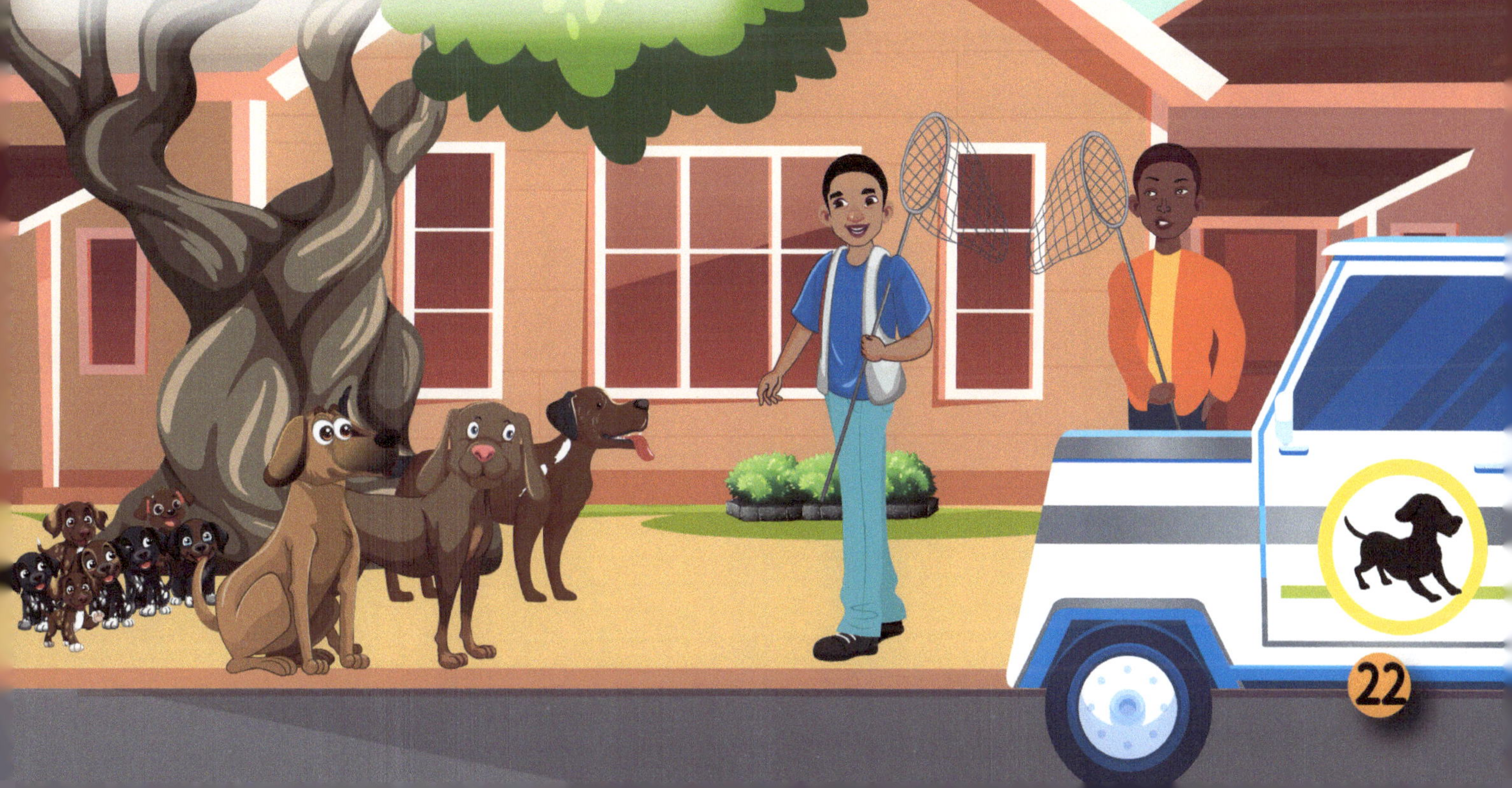

When the truck came to a stop, Pet and Danny heard dogs barking; they were each put into a cage. That night, Danny did not sleep; his mind was on Ruff. Ruff was like family to him. Danny couldn't even remember all that happened that night; all he remembered was the fight, and then everything after that happened so quickly that it was all a blur. The next day, Danny enquired of another one of the dogs what manner of place it was. The dog responded, "Don't be afraid; the humans here are nice. They take care of you really nicely too. They call it the Dog Haven, but I call it Dog Heaven!" Then a man came in a white coat and took the seven pups. Pet began to bark out of control. Danny tried to get her attention, but she refused to be calmed. Then a lady in a white coat came with a needle and put it into Pet. She quickly fell to the ground. Danny began to bark loudly and hit himself against the cage. One of the other dogs shouted across the room, "Hey, Newby! Settle down! These people won't harm you; that stuff is just gonna let her sleep for a while. I've been here for ten years, and these people ain't been nothing but good to me. So, calm down, man." Danny laid down a bit.

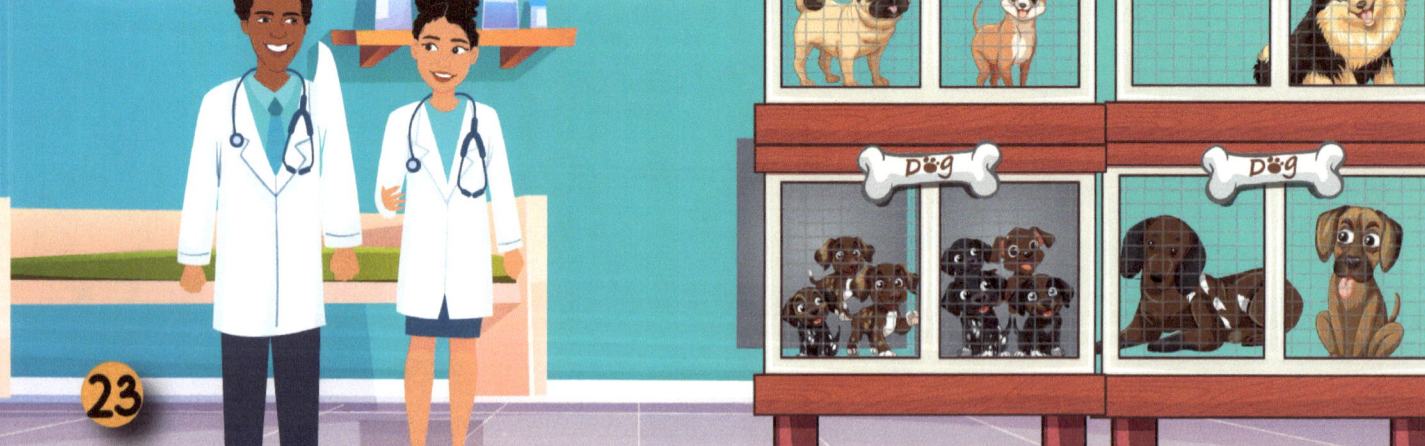

A few hours later, Pet woke up. Danny asked how she felt. She said she was a little drowsy, but she was fine. A little while later, the pups came back happy. Then some men came and opened Danny's cage and some other dogs' cages. So Danny asked what was happening. Another dog shouted, "The humans call it exercise; you will enjoy it! Just do what you see the rest of us do!" Danny observed as the humans led them around an open area, and all the dogs ran in a single line. Then they put the dogs in a circle, and a human threw a stick, and each dog would catch it in his mouth and run to the human. The human would take the stick and put something into the dog's mouth. When it was Danny's turn, he jumped, caught the stick, and brought it to the human. The human pat him on his head and gave him something that tasted quite yummy. Days went by, and Pet and Danny grew to enjoy their new life, and all the pups were happy.

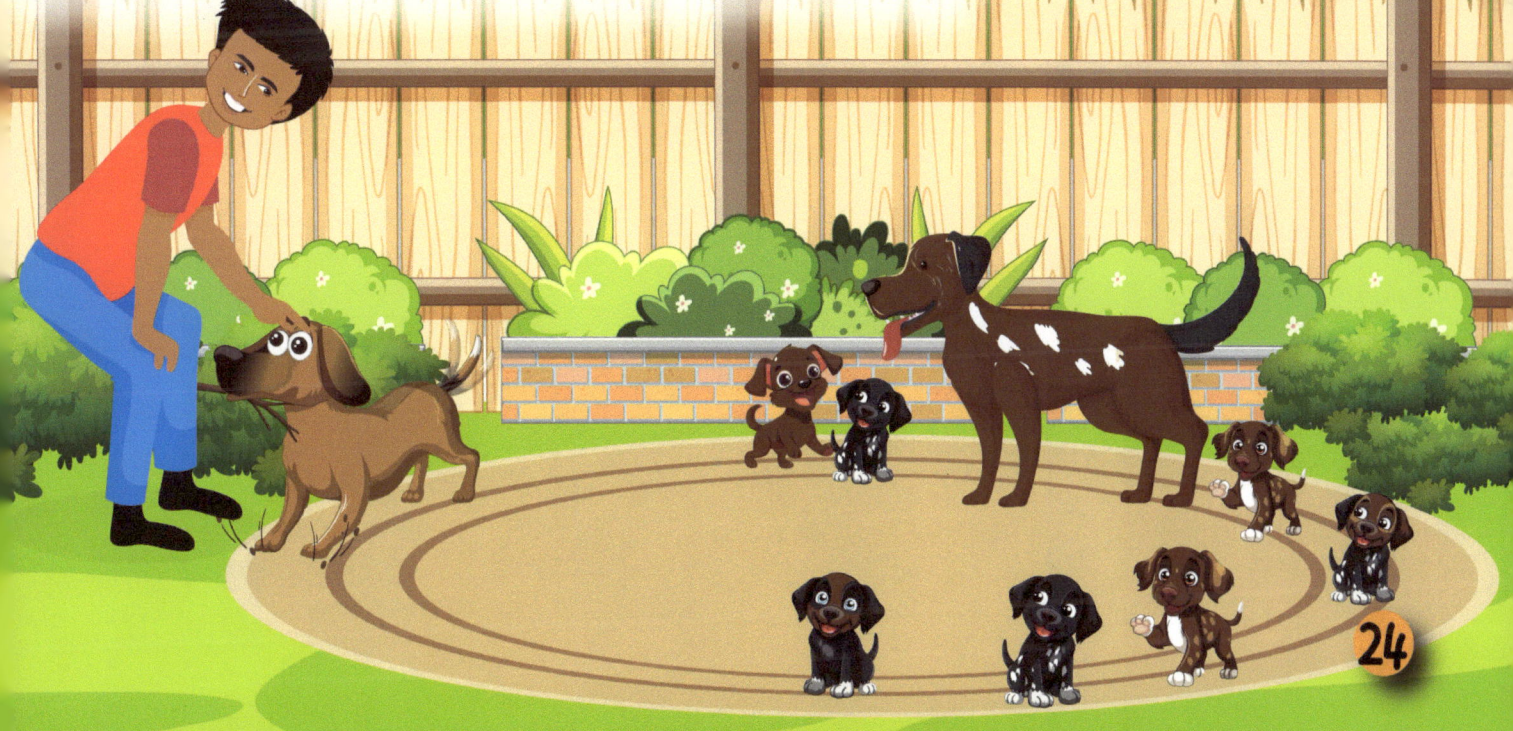

One day, some humans came; Danny had never seen them before. But he noticed all the dogs were acting strange, jumping, barking, and chasing their tails. So Danny asked the dog beside him what was happening and why he wasn't doing like the other dogs. The dog responded, "It's adoption day. That's when human families come in here; they look at each dog, choose one, and take them home. But I never get chosen; I'm blind in one eye and most people don't want a blind dog. But if you want to go, you can do like the other dogs. I'm fine. I'm just gonna lay here. This place is good enough for me." Danny decided to sit this one out. Then a little girl came in that reminded him of Sheila. He jumped up and began to bark. She came over and smiled at him. Then she walked to another dog's cage and chose the other dog. Danny was happy; nonetheless, he just wished Ruff was there with him to experience this life.

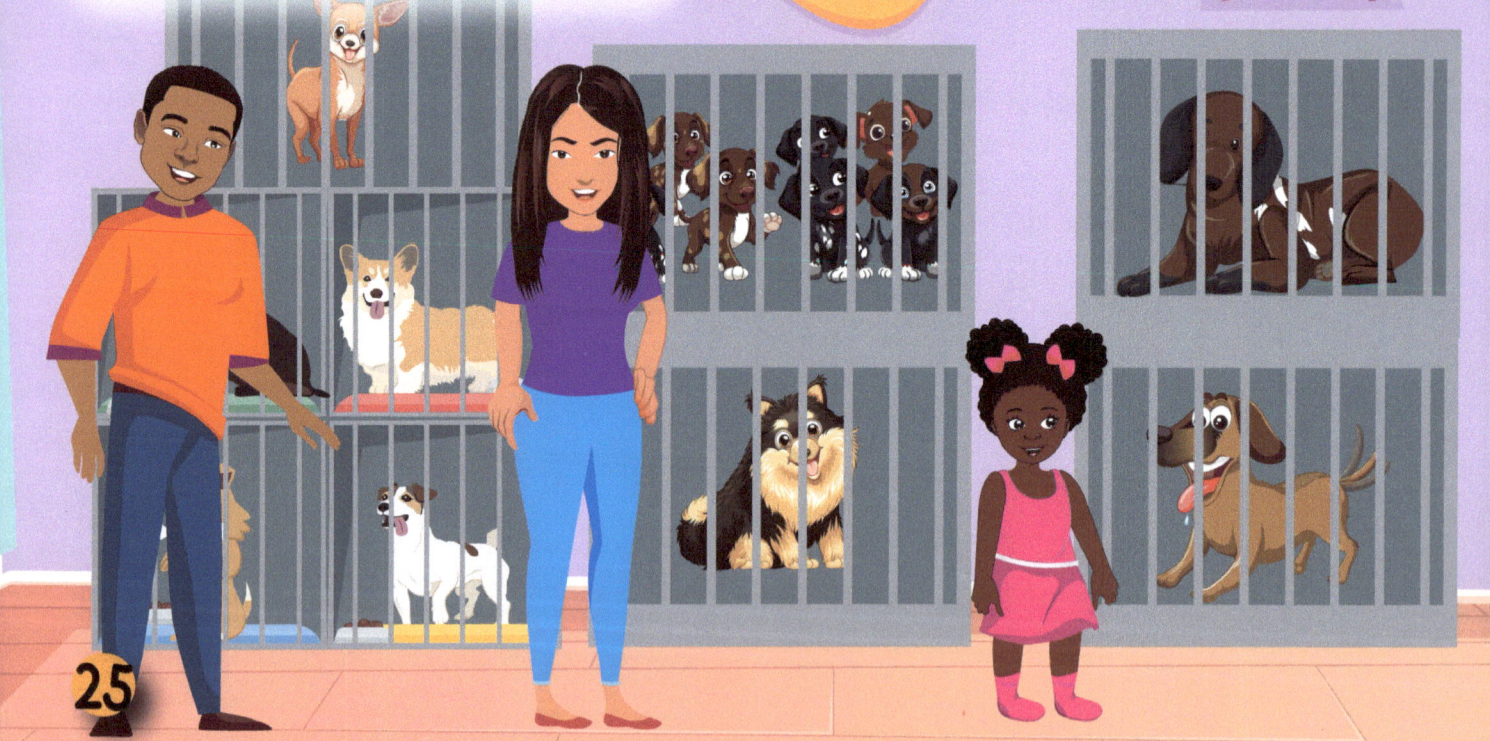

Danny grew to love his new life. He even had a favourite human who he would do tricks for, and she would give him extra treats. Then one day, a truck came in, and some of the dogs were being boarded along with their cage. Then Danny's favourite human came over, gave him a treat, and said goodbye. He began to panic. He did not want to go. He barked and hit himself against the cage. The man in the white coat came and injected him with a needle, and he fell asleep. A while later, he woke up and barely opened his eyes. When he looked, he saw a plane, and all the cages were being loaded in. He was still drowsy; he wanted to stay awake, but he couldn't. The next time he woke up, he was surrounded by people with smiles on their faces. A human in a white jacket looked inside his eyes, ears, and mouth with a bright light. They stuck him with a needle, but this time, it did not make him sleepy.

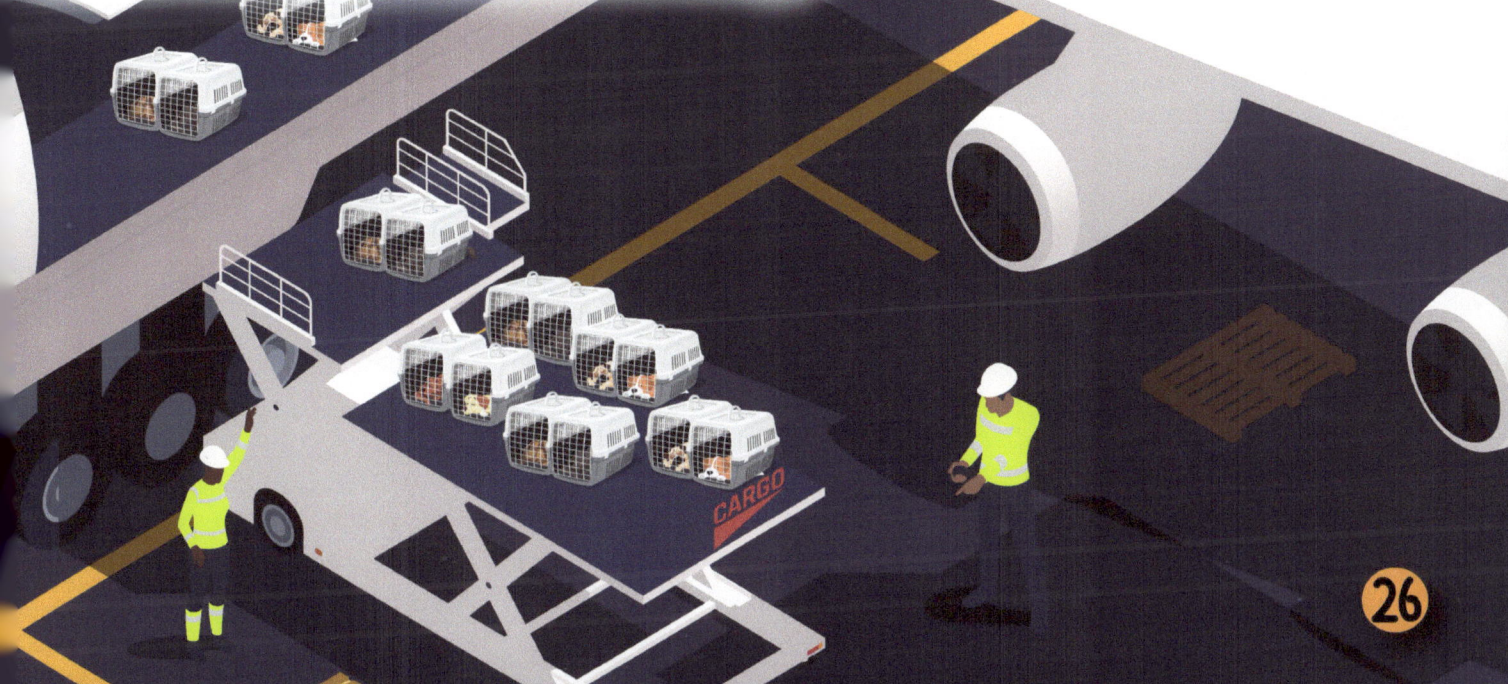

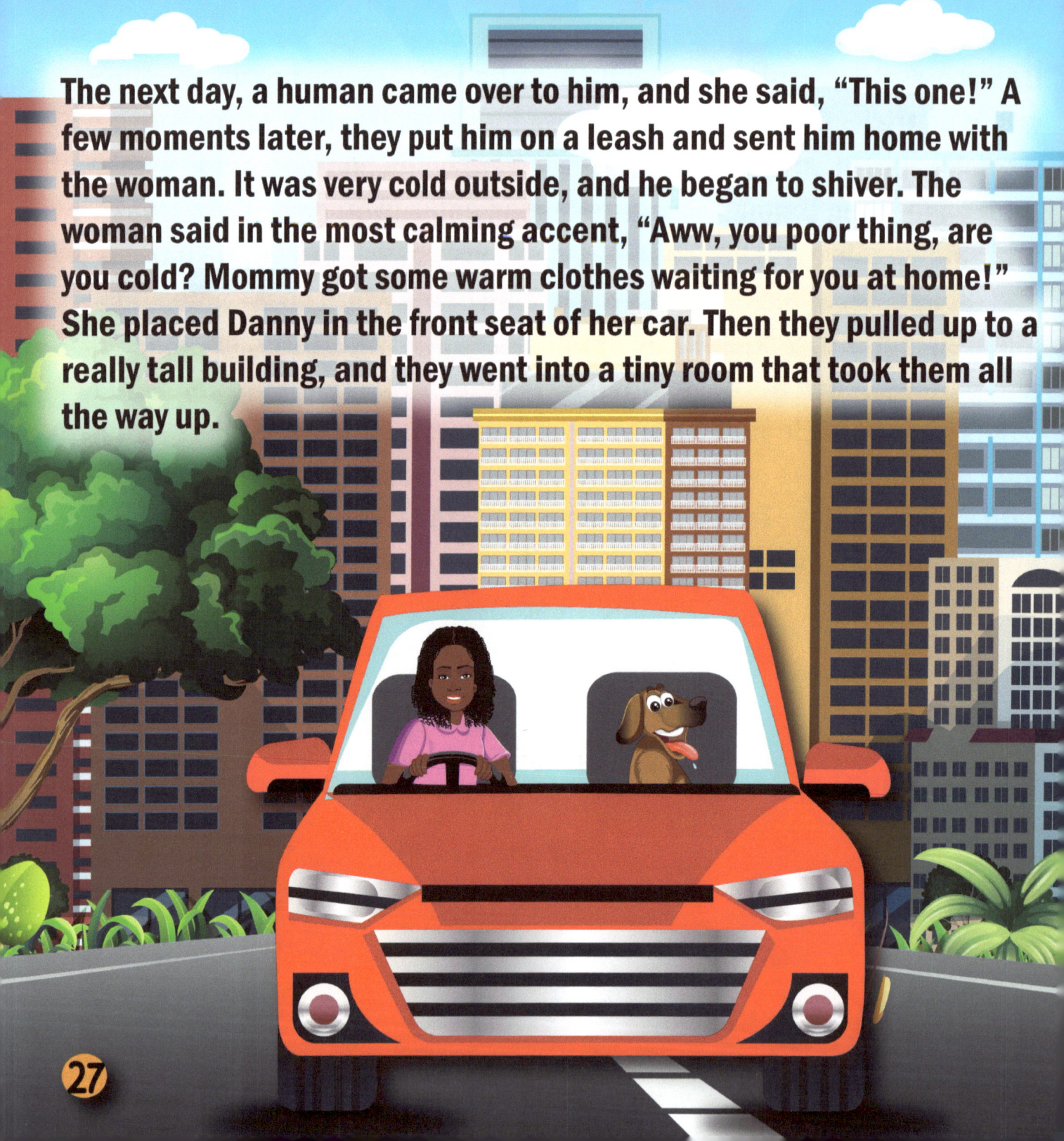

The next day, a human came over to him, and she said, "This one!" A few moments later, they put him on a leash and sent him home with the woman. It was very cold outside, and he began to shiver. The woman said in the most calming accent, "Aww, you poor thing, are you cold? Mommy got some warm clothes waiting for you at home!" She placed Danny in the front seat of her car. Then they pulled up to a really tall building, and they went into a tiny room that took them all the way up.

Then the woman opened the door and said, "We're home!" Danny stepped in and looked around in awe. It was just like he imagined. He sat and observed the lady; she had a pretty face, a pretty smile, and a pretty voice. She said, "What shall I call you?" The woman said, "Rover…" Danny growled. She said, "You don't like that, huh?" And she continued through a number of names, then she said, "Danny," and Danny jumped and wagged his tail. They sat and watched television, then she took Danny to sleep in her bed. Danny was so excited. The next day, she put him in a jacket, took him for a ride in her car, and brought him to a pet store. Then she said, I have a surprise for you! Then she presented a beautiful collar with the letters D-A-N-N-Y. Danny jumped with excitement. He even got his own bowl and bed. When he got home, the woman bathed him, gave him a meal, and they sat to watch television again. Danny was happy, and then he said to himself, "I wish Ruff would have lived to experience this, so he could see that dreams do come true."

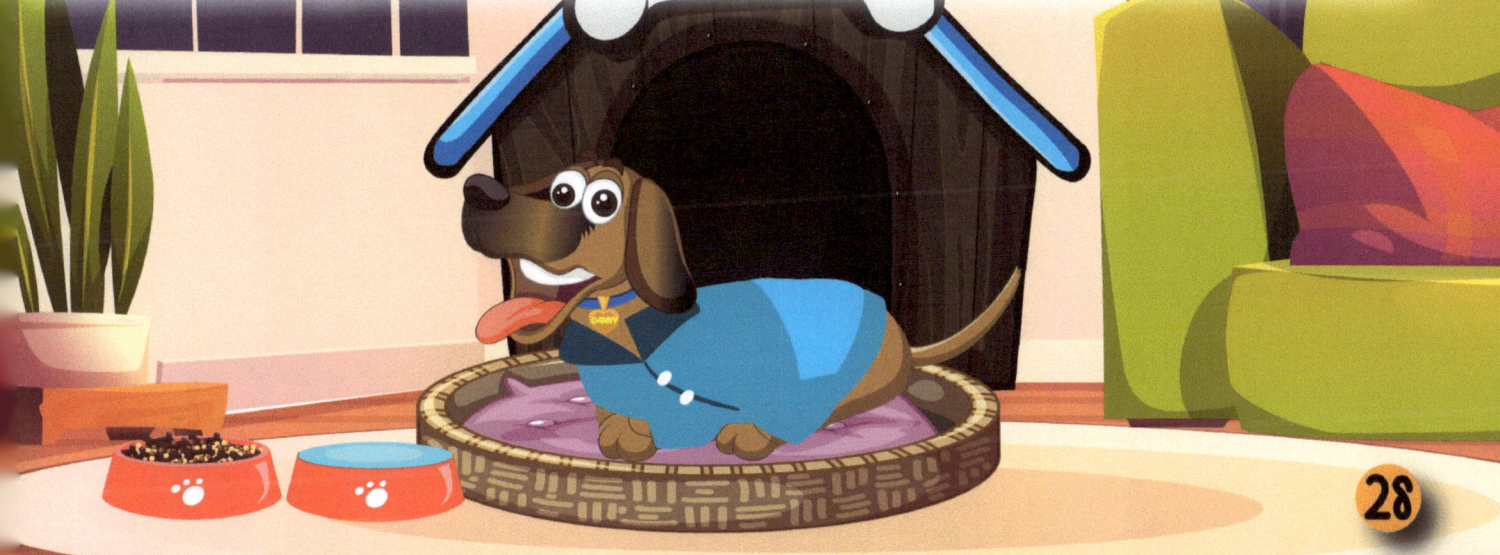

Meanwhile, back in Jamaica, word on the street was that dogs had gone on a plane to Canada. Ruff had formed another pack of The Jammings, and he had a rule that they should never talk about unrealistic things. But one of the dogs said, "Boss, it's true," and showed him a picture on a newspaper in the dumps. Ruff was surprised and grabbed it. When he looked, it was a picture of his long-lost friend, Danny. He shouted to the others, "Hey, look, this is that dreamer boy I told you guys about, and look, it's Pet!" Ruff sat back and wept. He was happy to know his friends were alive.

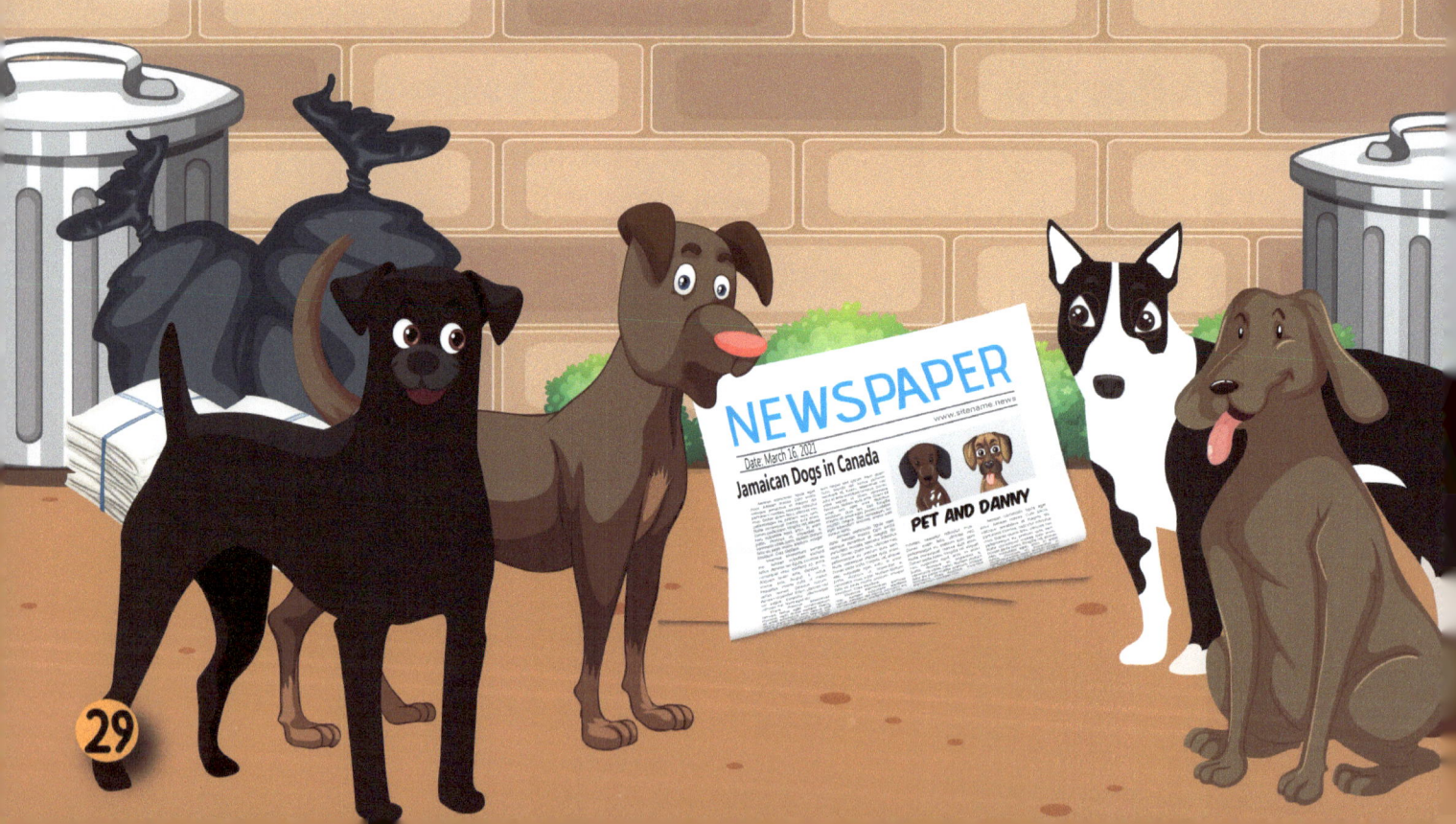

*Dear* _____,

Always remember, dreams do come true; all you have to do is believe in yourself and believe in your dreams. Don't let anyone cause you to not pursue your dreams.

Your picture here

*I can do all things through Christ who strengthens me. (Philippians 4:13)*

www.ingramcontent.com/pod-product-compliance
Lightning Source LLC
Chambersburg PA
CBHW051824210526
45473CB00005B/1735